Susan

Cook the Love up or
on "HIGH"

Live, Love, Eat

Simon Gault

+6421999893
Simon @simongault.com

SIMON GAULT began his food career at the age of 16 at Antoine's in Auckland. After travelling to England, where he worked in Prue Leith's London restaurant and the Michelin-starred Thornbury Castle, he returned to New Zealand to open Bell House – the first of his many award-winning restaurants. Today his restaurant empire includes Euro and Jervois Steak House in Auckland, Pravda and Shed 5 in Wellington, Bistro Lago in Taupo and a second Jervois Steak House in Queenstown. Simon has built a loyal following through his innovative and stylish menus offering everything from tapas to seafood and steak. He is a judge of *MasterChef New Zealand* and in demand for regular live cooking demonstrations.

www.simongault.com

For Mum and Dad,
my best friends and staunchest critics

SIMON GAULT
homemade

Photography
Kieran Scott

PENGUIN BOOKS

CONTENTS

MY STORY

Some of my earliest memories are of my mum, Ellerie, and my dad, Bryan, in the kitchen cooking together. Dad was an airline pilot and spent a lot of time away from the family, but whenever he was home he'd be alongside Mum cooking and talking about food. In my family there was always excitement about food and so it was something that interested me from a very young age. Having my friends over could be a bit of a nightmare because it was totally normal for us to be eating interesting things like calves' liver or chicken stuffed with oysters, which not many other kids would have encountered.

Dad's mum had a café bakery in Paraparaumu, which he had to help out in as a boy. Consequently Dad became a great baker – and he still is. He's also a keen gardener so there are always plenty of fresh vegetables on offer – his recipes for cooked cabbage and silverbeet are so good I've included them in this book. In fact, many of the recipes you'll find on the following pages are based on the things Mum and Dad have cooked over the years and I grew up eating. They have stayed with me and stood the test of time – always the hallmark of a really great dish. Others have been influenced by time I've spent travelling or working overseas, and one or two you'll find on the menu of my Auckland restaurant Euro. Eating and cooking in Italy, France and Spain taught me that every great dish starts with the best ingredients – not necessarily the most expensive, but those that carry the extra flavour. Vine-ripened tomatoes, good-quality olive oil, Parmigiano-Reggiano, even day-old crusty Italian bread that can be used as a base for panzanella (bread and tomato salad).

There's a photo of me cooking at a family barbecue at the age of eight dressed in a chef's apron and hat, and I think I always knew that I wanted to become a chef and have my own restaurant. On family holidays I'd find my way into the hotel kitchen, and then I'd lie awake at night designing the kitchen I would one day have in my restaurant. At age 12 I got a job helping to wash dishes in a local Italian restaurant. I don't think I even cared if they paid me – I was just so excited to be there.

When I was supposed to be studying for School Certificate I went down to Wellington to meet a friend of my parents, the 'galloping gourmet' Des Britten. He got me an interview with Tony Astle, owner of the legendary Auckland restaurant

Antoine's, and at 16 I started working there. Tony was the 'godfather' of New Zealand cuisine and he's still someone I look up to. In Tony's kitchen I learnt that nothing less than perfection was acceptable. If you cut a piece of eye fillet too thick, then it came flying back at you across the kitchen. I think that experience really set me up for my restaurant career because it instilled in me the desire to always find that extra 'five per cent magic'.

Travelling to London at the age of 19 (during the coldest winter since 1877) was the beginning of some incredible international cooking experiences. I started as a commis chef in the kitchen of Leith's restaurant before talking my way into a job in the kitchen of the revered British chef Kenneth Bell at his famous Thornbury Castle, the first restaurant in Britain to earn a Michelin star. The ingredients they used there were incredible. The cheesemonger would pull up with a vanload of cheeses; there were piles of fresh truffles from Italy; and the award-winning cellar held more than 32,000 bottles of wine. I was in my element. I got to cook with things that you never got to handle unless you worked in a place like that – ingredients that I'd certainly never seen back in New Zealand. It was an awesome experience.

When my visa ran out I came back to Auckland and at the age of 22 I was ready to start my own restaurant. With Mum as my business partner I bought the old Bell Farmhouse in Howick Colonial Village and set up Bell House – one of Auckland's few fine-dining restaurants at the time. In those days most of the flash restaurants were in the centre of town so it took a while to make it onto the map, but then the reviews and awards started rolling in and I was able to get suppliers to import some of the ingredients I'd encountered overseas. Back then it was a challenge to find an alternative to iceberg lettuce, let alone some good French cheeses. It's hard to believe these days, I know, when you can find excellent Parmigiano-Reggiano, Parma ham and aged balsamic vinegar in high-quality food stores all over the country.

I have a lot to thank my family for. In those early days, everyone was involved – helping with the set-up, washing dishes, offering me advice and acting as my staunchest critics. I'm lucky that my family are honest enough to tell me what they like, and that has always been a key thing for me. If there is something they don't like then I certainly sit up and listen, which is probably why I've turned to Gault family favourites as the basis for this cookbook.

When I moved on from Bell House I was keen to move into town. My next restaurant, Gaults on Quay, was one of the first restaurants to set up in Auckland's Viaduct Basin. I wasn't even 30 and, to be honest, I almost got it wrong. With the Whitbread Round the World yacht race fleet in port we were doing up to 800 meals a day. It was too many to be in control. Money was flowing through the tills but we were doing a pretty terrible job of managing the restaurant. Then the Whitbread fleet left town and the crowds stopped coming. I was so close to going bust that I was using leftover egg whites to make meringue roulades to sell to local cafés. It taught me a valuable lesson about management, as well as the need to embrace change – something that has been a constant throughout my career. We refitted the bar, adapted the menu and once again we were cranking. The America's Cup was huge for us – I remember the day we won the Cup in San Diego like it was yesterday. With the America's Cup racing coming to New Zealand, the Viaduct Basin was suddenly the place to be and in 1998 I was offered a lot of money for Gaults. So here I was, in my early thirties, two restaurants along and with a bit of a reputation as the 'young kid on the block'. I was thinking where to next when I met the TV producer and creator of the *Idol* television series, Simon Fuller, who was holidaying in New Zealand. He hired me to cook for him during a week on a boat in the Bay of Islands and we hit it off, and before I knew it he'd invited me to join him for a year's sabbatical in Italy. It was during that year away that I learnt the magic of Italian food. We were staying in these glorious villas, and I'm not very good at sitting about with my feet up, so I'd head for the kitchen and spend time with the chefs cooking family-style dishes. We'd go to the markets and down to the wharf to get prawns and tuna straight off the fishing boats. It was an incredible experience, and once again it taught me the value of working with great ingredients. I still go overseas to look and learn, and for me that means rolling up to a restaurant in Sicily and asking for an apron, not visiting some flash resort for 10 days' downtime.

Now, with my import business Sous Chef I bring more than 300 food products into New Zealand. Yes, I import salt from Australia because I happen to think that New Zealand doesn't produce particularly good salt. But if I hadn't imported Italian buffalo mozzarella, no one would have started making it here and we'd still be eating the horrible rubbery stuff. So now I'm quite happy to cook with the mozzarella made by Clevedon Valley Buffalo Company, just down the road from where I live. It's not about cooking only with imported ingredients. My ethos is about cooking with what tastes best – great anchovies, free-range bacon, good olive oil – whatever it is that will give a dish that 'five per cent magic'.

With a bunch of restaurants to look after, these days having time to cook at home is the best thing. That's when I get into the kitchen and just play. Like most people, time for me is a luxury, which is why the recipes in this book are mostly about delivering an impressive result without too much effort. Most importantly, they are recipes to be enjoyed, not stressed over. I still cook some dishes that don't turn out quite as I'd hoped, and I've been a chef for more than 20 years. Sometimes my wife Katrina won't like one element of a dish – and generally she'll be right. I'm still learning. I don't think that will ever stop.

What I can promise is that the recipes for starters, mains, sides and desserts you'll find in the following pages have been at the heart of some memorable Gault family meals. I hope they will become favourites with your friends and family too.

Simon

starters

ONION RINGS WITH HORSERADISH MAYO

These make a perfect snack to serve with a drink when guests arrive. The Horseradish Mayo is also great as an accompaniment to steak.

Serves 2–4

1 cup flour

6 eggs, beaten

80g Parmigiano-Reggiano, grated

200g panko breadcrumbs

4 large onions, cut into 5mm slices

canola oil for frying

Horseradish Mayo

6 tbsp mayonnaise

2 tbsp fresh grated horseradish

Place the flour and eggs in separate bowls. Combine the Parmigiano-Reggiano and panko crumbs in another bowl and set aside.

Separate the onion rings, then dip into the flour, followed by the egg, then the panko crumbs. Place in the freezer for 15–20 minutes.

In a large saucepan or deep-fryer, heat the oil to 165°C. Deep-fry the onion rings in batches until golden, using a tea strainer to scoop out any bits left in the oil between batches. Drain on paper towels and season with salt.

Combine the mayonnaise and horseradish and place in a small serving dish.

Serve the onion rings on a round platter with the Horseradish Mayo placed in a bowl in the centre.

Simon says

You will find fresh horseradish in good vegetable shops when in season. Once grated, use horseradish immediately or mix it with vinegar, otherwise it loses its pungency and becomes bitter.

SHRIMP FRITTERS

You will find these crisp little fritters, called tortillitas de camarones in Spanish, being sold on every windswept street corner in the port of Cádiz in southern Spain. They source the smallest shrimps they can find, but in my recipe I have used prawn cutlets. Chickpea flour and good Spanish paprika are the secret ingredients that make these fritters unforgettable.

Serves 8

1 tbsp self-raising flour

1¼ cups chickpea flour

¾ tsp bicarbonate of soda

1½ tsp flaky salt

100ml water

1 egg

90ml extra virgin olive oil

1½ tsp Spanish smoked paprika

½ tsp cayenne pepper

zest of 1 lemon

3 tbsp very finely chopped onion

4 tbsp finely chopped curly parsley

330g raw prawn cutlets (defrosted and roughly chopped) or baby shrimps

100ml olive oil for frying

lemon wedges to serve

Sift the flours, bicarbonate of soda and salt into a bowl. Mix the water and egg, add the olive oil and stir to combine, then gradually blend into the flour mixture to form a thin batter. Add the paprika, cayenne pepper, lemon zest, onion, parsley and prawns or shrimps and mix well.

Heat the olive oil in a frying-pan. When it begins to shimmer (see note page 74), drop in a large spoonful of batter for each fritter, frying 3 at a time (if you crowd the pan, the oil temperature will drop and you will end up with oily fritters). Fry until golden and crisp on both sides and cooked through. Ensure the batter is well spread out so the fritters will be crisp all the way through. Remove from the pan and drain on paper towels. Serve hot in stacks with lemon wedges.

Simon says

The perfect dip for these fritters is to take your favourite mayonnaise and add some Spanish smoked paprika and a touch of garlic. This makes a paprika aïoli.

CHICKEN LIVER AND SHERRY TARTS

These tarts are best served warm. I like to serve them as a family-style entrée in the centre of the table for people to help themselves, or as a buffet-style starter served with napkins. Use the shortcrust pastry from the Treacle Tarts (page 206) to make the tart cases.

Makes 24 tartlets

500g chicken livers

3 Spanish green olives, pitted and finely chopped

1 hard-boiled egg yolk, mashed

¼ cup finely chopped curly parsley

100g butter

1½ spring onions, finely chopped

4 tsp flour

¾ cup chicken stock

3 tbsp dry Spanish sherry

6 button mushrooms, washed, trimmed and thinly sliced

24 tartlet pastry cases (storebought or see recipe page 206)

Pick over the livers and remove any small green pieces (these are very bitter) and chop the livers into small pieces.

Combine the olives, egg yolk and parsley, and set aside.

Heat the butter in a frying-pan and when hot add the livers and brown quickly. Do not cook completely. Remove to a warm platter and season with a little salt.

Add the spring onions to the pan and sauté until soft. Add the flour and cook quickly, stirring, then add the chicken stock and sherry and stir constantly until the mixture is thickened and smooth.

Season with salt and pepper and add the mushrooms. Cover and simmer for 4 minutes (the filling can be prepared ahead to this point).

Return the livers to the sauce and cook for a couple of minutes or until cooked through.

Pile the filling into the tartlet cases and garnish with the olive, egg and parsley mixture to serve.

Simon says

When making the short pastry cases for the tartlets, follow the steps on page 206 up to rolling out the pastry to a thickness of 2–3mm. Use the pastry to line 24 x 6cm tartlet tins. Rest in the fridge for 30 minutes. Blind bake in an oven preheated to 185°C for 15 minutes. Remove tartlet cases from the oven, take out the baking paper and rice, and bake for another 5–7 minutes, or until pastry is golden. Remove from the oven and allow to cool.

ROAST GARLIC SOUP

Lots of people are a bit timid about eating garlic, but roasting garlic gives it a lovely nutty flavour, and I can think of nothing better than a steaming bowl of this soup as an entrée to a hearty meal or for lunch on a wintry day. Serve this with kumara bread. Sensational!

Serves 6

16 whole heads garlic

2 tbsp extra virgin olive oil

2 tbsp butter

½ onion, chopped

1 leek (white and light-green part only), well washed and chopped

750g potatoes, peeled and diced

1.1 litres chicken or vegetable stock

¾ cup milk

2 tbsp cream

12 slices kumara bread or ciabatta, chargrilled

Preheat the oven to 190°C. Prepare 8 squares of aluminium foil large enough to wrap 2 heads each of the garlic. Slice the top 3cm from each garlic head and place 2 heads in the centre of each foil square. Season with salt and freshly ground white pepper and drizzle with olive oil. Carefully fold the foil to enclose the garlic heads, place in a roasting pan and roast for 20 minutes or until the garlic is soft when squeezed.

Meanwhile, in a saucepan over medium heat melt the butter, add the onion and leek and cook until soft. Add the potatoes and sauté for 3 minutes. Add the stock, bring to a simmer and cook until the potatoes are fork tender (about 20 minutes).

Remove the garlic from the oven when cooked and set aside to cool. Carefully squeeze the garlic from the skins into a bowl, being sure to remove any stray pieces of skin that fall in. Add the garlic and milk to the saucepan and stir to combine.

Transfer the soup to a blender and purée until smooth. Season with salt and pepper to taste. Pour into 6 bowls, garnish with a swirl of cream and serve with grilled bread. I used kumara bread.

CHIPOTLE MUSSELS

These make fantastic finger-food. They are something that I always serve at a barbecue. Tabasco chipotle sauce, made with smoked chillies, is available in specialty food stores and good supermarkets. Butter and chipotle – it really doesn't get any easier.

Serves 6

2 cups white wine

½ onion, sliced

1kg mussels

50g butter

1 tbsp Tabasco chipotle sauce

Heat a large saucepan, add the wine and onion, place the lid on and cook until the onion is soft, then add the mussels. Replace the lid and steam until the mussels just start to open.

In a separate saucepan melt the butter and add the Tabasco chipotle sauce.

Take the mussel meat from the shells and remove the tongues and beards, then add to the melted butter sauce and mix to coat. Reheat the mussels in the butter sauce, then place on the shells with a little of the sauce and serve.

Simon says

Make sure you discard any mussels that do not open during cooking. To debeard the mussels, pull the threads down towards the pointy end of the shell, discarding the brown foot and any muscle attached to the shell.

ANTIPASTO DIPS

Everybody loves dips before a meal, and here are three that really have that X factor. Each is a great flavour combo in itself and together they make a sensational tasting platter with vegetable crudités.

4 tbsp olive oil

½ onion, finely chopped

1 tsp finely chopped garlic

1 long red chilli,
seeded and finely sliced

¼ cup toasted pine nuts

2 tsp balsamic vinegar

½ cup roasted and finely chopped
red capsicum (see page 111)

1 tsp salt

SPICY ROAST RED CAPSICUM DIP

Heat half the oil in a frying-pan over medium heat and sauté the onion, garlic and chilli until soft. Add the remaining ingredients, including the remaining oil, and stir to combine. Place the mixture in a food processor and purée until still slightly chunky.

¼ cup mayonnaise

½ tsp finely chopped garlic

2 tsp finely chopped
flat-leaf parsley

3 tbsp cream

1 tsp lemon juice

100g blue cheese, crumbled

¼ cup mascarpone

BLUE CHEESE DIP

Place all the ingredients except the mascarpone in a blender and purée until smooth (if the mayonnaise is runny, you may need to omit the cream and add extra mayonnaise instead). Remove and stir in the mascarpone.

½ cup peeled, chopped and
roasted orange kumara

125g cream cheese

seeds of 1 vanilla pod

¼ tsp each ground ginger,
turmeric and Spanish sweet
smoked paprika

ROAST SWEET POTATO AND GINGER DIP

Place all the ingredients in a blender and purée until smooth. Season with salt to taste.

EASY FISHCAKES

Smoked paprika is the secret weapon in these, while panko crumbs give a light, crisp crust. You could replace the fresh fish here with smoked fish. Serve these fishcakes with Chipotle Mayo – also great with roasted potatoes.

Serves 4

2 cups milk

1¼ cups water

¼ tsp ground white pepper

300g skinned and boned fresh white-fleshed fish

300g potatoes (preferably Agria), peeled, boiled until well cooked and passed through a sieve

2 tbsp chopped curly parsley

¼ tsp Spanish hot smoked paprika, plus extra to garnish

¾ cup flour

3 eggs, beaten

80g panko breadcrumbs

4 tbsp olive oil

4 tbsp butter

Chipotle Mayo

250ml mayonnaise

Tabasco chipotle sauce to taste

lemon wedges to serve

In a large saucepan, place the milk, water and white pepper and bring to a simmer. Add the fish and poach until just cooked (poach fish gently; do not boil or the fish will be tough), then drain, discarding the liquid, and allow to cool.

Flake the fish and combine with the potato, parsley and smoked paprika. Season well with salt to taste. Refrigerate until chilled, which makes the mixture easer to mould.

Divide the mixture into 8 and form each portion into a ball, then gently press to flatten. Place the flour, eggs and breadcrumbs in 3 separate bowls, then coat the fishcakes first in flour then egg then the crumbs. In a large frying-pan heat the olive oil until starting to shimmer (see note page 74), add the butter and then place the fishcakes on the melting butter. Fry the cakes until golden brown on both sides and cooked through.

Combine the mayonnaise and Tabasco chipotle sauce in a small bowl and top with a pinch of smoked paprika. Sprinkle the fishcakes with a little flaky salt, and serve with lemon wedges and the Chipotle Mayo alongside.

Simon says

I use the Kewpie brand of mayonnaise, a Japanese brand that is particularly creamy and delicious.

MUSSEL SALAD

This is an old-school salad made with rice, so it can also make a hearty meal for 2–3 people. It's a firm favourite with the Gault family.

Serves 6

120g button mushrooms, washed, trimmed and thickly sliced

2 tbsp lemon juice

⅔ cup white wine

½ cup water

1.8kg mussels, scrubbed

½ cup chicken stock (you may need less)

120g jasmine rice

1 shallot, finely chopped

3 tbsp olive oil

½ bay leaf

1 stalk celery, peeled

60ml cream

1 tbsp finely chopped curly parsley

Combine the mushrooms, lemon juice and some freshly ground black pepper in a bowl and leave to marinate for 2 hours or more.

In a large saucepan place the wine and water. Cover the pan, bring to a simmer, then add the mussels, cover and simmer until the shells just open. Transfer the mussels to a bowl with a slotted spoon. Strain the liquid into a measuring jug and make up to 300ml with chicken stock.

Rinse the rice under cold running water and set aside to drain. In a medium saucepan, sauté the shallot in olive oil until translucent, then add the rice. Pour in the combined mussel liquor and stock, bring to the boil, add the bay leaf, cover the pan and cook until the rice is tender and the stock absorbed (8–10 minutes).

Meanwhile, cut the celery into batons about 2.5cm long. Set aside.

Take the mussels from their shells and remove the beards and tongues. Mix the mussels with the mushrooms. Turn the rice into a separate bowl to cool. When the rice is quite cold, add the celery, mussels and mushrooms and mix with a fork, taste for seasoning and then add the cream. Pile onto entrée dishes and sprinkle with chopped parsley.

BREAD DUMPLINGS AND TOMATOES

Known as poor man's dumplings, these make a great vegetarian dish. The secret weapon is the addition of Manchego cheese to the dumpling mix. And good-quality canned Italian tomatoes for the sauce make all the difference.

Serves 4

2 tbsp extra virgin olive oil, plus extra to serve

1 onion, thinly sliced

1 cup white wine

400g whole, peeled, canned Italian tomatoes

4 tbsp chopped fresh basil, plus sprigs for garnish

7 thick slices day-old ciabatta, crusts removed

4 eggs, beaten

100g Manchego, grated

canola oil for frying

Heat the olive oil in a saucepan over medium heat, add the onion and sauté for 3 minutes until soft. Add the white wine and simmer over medium heat until reduced by half, then add the tomatoes, break up with a spoon and cook for a further 10 minutes. Transfer the mixture to a blender and purée until smooth. Return the sauce to the saucepan, season with salt and freshly ground black pepper and keep warm. When ready to serve, bring back to the boil and at the last minute add 2 tablespoons of the chopped basil.

Pulse the bread in a food processor to coarse crumbs, then transfer to a bowl. Add the eggs, cheese and remaining basil and season with salt and black pepper. Use your hands to mix to a dough.

Into a large frying-pan over medium heat pour canola oil to a depth of about 5cm and heat to 180°C. Form the dough into golf-ball-sized dumplings. Carefully lower into the hot oil and fry for 10 minutes or until golden all over. You may have to do this in batches. Remove the dumplings from the oil using a slotted spoon and drain on paper towels. Stir the sauce and divide between 4 bowls, place the dumplings in the sauce and garnish with a sprig of basil and a drizzle of olive oil.

POTATO SOUP

This soup tastes so fantastic it's hard to believe it's made with the humble potato. It's the addition of Colman's mustard that gives it the edge. Dijon or wholegrain mustard would also work really well.

Serves 6

4 rashers rindless lean
bacon, diced

50ml olive oil

4 leeks (white part only),
well washed and thinly sliced

¼ cup chopped onion

2 tbsp flour

1.8 litres chicken stock

750g large potatoes,
peeled and thinly sliced

2 tsp Colman's
prepared mustard

2 egg yolks, beaten

1 cup sour cream

2 tbsp finely chopped chives

12 slices ciabatta

Sauté the bacon in a deep saucepan for 5 minutes. Add the olive oil, leek and onion and sauté for 3 minutes. Stir in the flour, then slowly add the stock, stirring constantly until thickened. Add the potatoes and simmer for 35 minutes.

Remove from the heat, pour the mixture into a blender and blend until smooth and creamy. Return the soup to the saucepan and bring to the boil. Add the mustard and adjust the seasoning to taste.

Combine the egg yolks and sour cream and place a little in each of 6 small serving dishes. Pour the remainder into the soup and lightly stir in. Ladle the soup into 6 bowls, arrange on plates with the dishes of sour cream mixture alongside and sprinkle the soup with chopped chives.

Serve the soup with fresh ciabatta, or brush the slices of ciabatta with olive oil and chargrill on a grill or barbecue.

PARMESAN PROFITEROLES

Ideal finger-food for parties, these are good served warm or cold but have to be eaten on the day they're made. While profiteroles sound fancy, they are easier to make than you might think. Be sure to have the eggs and flour at room temperature, and you don't need to use a piping bag – I like the more rustic look achieved by placing teaspoonfuls of mixture on the baking tray or simply rolling it into balls. Whether for a fancy dinner party or a laid-back brunch, simple Parmesan profiteroles will surely keep your guests blissfully satisfied.

Makes approximately 40

2 cups water

60g butter

pinch of freshly grated nutmeg

2 cups flour

4 large eggs

1¼ cups freshly grated
Parmigiano-Reggiano

Preheat the oven to 180°C. In a saucepan over high heat bring the water to the boil. Add the butter, nutmeg and a pinch of salt. When the butter melts, lower the heat and add the flour, stirring with a wooden spoon until the dough forms into a ball. Remove from the heat and set aside to cool for about 3 minutes.

Place the dough in an electric mixer and add the eggs one at a time, beating well between each addition. Add the Parmigiano and mix until well combined. Divide the dough into walnut-sized balls, place on a baking sheet lined with baking paper and bake for 20–25 minutes or until the profiteroles are slightly golden. Remove from the oven and serve in a pile on a plate.

Simon says
Store eggs in their original carton so you can be sure of their best before date. Fresh eggs can be kept safely for 2–3 weeks in the refrigerator.

MARINATED SNAPPER SALAD

In Fiji you'll be served the classic Island dish of marinated fish in coconut milk. In my version, the addition of ginger and a pinch of nutmeg transforms it into something special. You could use any white-fleshed fish; the freshness is the key.

Serves 4

500g skinned and boned snapper fillets

225ml coconut cream

4 shallots, finely chopped

½ red capsicum, cored and finely chopped

½ cup lemon juice

2 tbsp chopped curly parsley

1 stalk celery, finely chopped

½ tsp grated fresh ginger

1 tsp salt

¾ tsp white pepper

pinch of nutmeg

iceberg lettuce leaves to serve

Cut the snapper into bite-sized pieces, place in a bowl, add the remaining ingredients except the lettuce and mix well.

Marinate for 4 hours in the fridge. Drain off the excess liquid and serve slightly chilled on individual lettuce leaves on a platter.

Simon says
When buying fresh fish look for the flesh to be bright and shiny. If buying a whole fish, the gills should be rich red and the eyes clear. Smell it. It should not smell too 'fishy'.

CUCUMBER AND CHICKEN LIVER PÂTÉ ROULADE

A bit like a fancy sushi roll, this makes an appealing hors d'oeuvre. Best of all, it's one of those dishes you can make ahead of time. Just cover the rolls with a damp tea towel and slice them when you're ready to serve. Make the crêpe batter ahead of time and let it rest for 2 hours before cooking. The thinner the crêpe the better; using a non-stick frying-pan helps. This recipe makes more pâté and crêpes than you need for the roulade, but both can be kept for another use.

Serves 6

Pâté

500g chicken livers

75g butter

1 large onion, finely chopped

2 cloves garlic, finely chopped

200g flat mushrooms, sliced

200ml cream

1 tbsp redcurrant jelly

1 tsp freshly ground black pepper

500g butter, softened

2 tbsp chopped flat-leaf parsley

Crêpes

1 cup flour

2 eggs

1 tbsp extra virgin olive oil

300ml milk

1 tbsp unsalted butter, melted

6 tsp olive oil

To assemble

¼ cucumber, peeled, seeded and cut into batons

sprigs of chervil or curly parsley to garnish

PÂTÉ

Pick over the livers and remove any small green pieces (these are very bitter). Melt the 75g butter in a saucepan, add the chicken livers and onion, and cook on medium heat for 8 minutes or until the livers are cooked and the onion soft. Add the garlic, mushrooms, cream, redcurrant jelly and black pepper. Continue cooking on medium heat until the cream has reduced by two-thirds.

Allow the liver mixture to cool, then place in a food processor, add the softened butter and parsley, season to taste with salt and blend to a smooth consistency.

CRÊPES

Combine the flour, eggs, extra virgin olive oil, milk and butter. Mix well and refrigerate for 2 hours to rest.

Heat 1 teaspoon of the olive oil in a crêpe pan or non-stick frying-pan until hot. Pour in enough mixture to cover the base of the pan. Cook until the crêpe is firm enough to turn with a pallet knife. The underside should be a light golden colour. Cook for a further 20 seconds. Remove from the pan and check that the crêpe is cooked through. Repeat to make 6 crêpes. The remaining crêpe mixture will keep for 2 days in an airtight container in the refrigerator.

Place the crêpes on a bench with a pallet knife. Smear 2 tablespoons of pâté over each crêpe, all the way to the edges. Place the cucumber in a line a third in from the edge of each crêpe. Roll up tightly. Keep at room temperature until ready to serve. Cut into pieces and garnish with sprigs of chervil or curly parsley and cracked pepper.

MENU
elegant spring barbecue

Spring is a great time to invite friends around for a 'here comes summer' barbecue.
A platter of dips that can be passed around is the ideal alternative to a sit-down entrée
for this kind of casual but elegant meal. Perfectly cooked tuna and buffalo mozzarella
make a wicked combination, and you can't go past new season's strawberries for dessert.

STARTER

Antipasto Dips
(page 28)

MAIN

Yellowfin Tuna and Buffalo Mozzarella Salad
(page 100)

DESSERT

Strawberries in Snow
(page 188)

ITALIAN SAUSAGE DUMPLINGS

This is basically an upmarket dumpling soup, based on one of my mum's recipes. I've flashed it up with some truffle oil and grated Parmigiano-Reggiano. Make the dumplings with your favourite sausages, which flavour the stock as they cook. If you like your dumplings spicy, add fresh chilli or chilli flakes to the sausage mix. These are perfect as an entrée or a main, depending on the number of dumplings served.

Serves 4

125g ciabatta

2 tbsp finely chopped curly parsley

2 eggs, beaten

70g Parmigiano-Reggiano, grated, plus extra to serve

200g Italian sausages, casings removed (I use pork and fennel sausages)

2 tbsp flour, plus ½ cup extra for dusting

2 litres chicken stock, plus 2 tbsp extra

extra virgin olive oil or truffle oil to serve

Cut the bread into small cubes and place in a food processor. Add the parsley, eggs and Parmigiano, and blend to combine. Crumble the sausages, add to the bread mixture and season with salt and freshly ground black pepper. Mix the flour and 2 tablespoons of the stock to form a paste, add to the processor and blend until all the ingredients are thoroughly combined, then set aside to rest for 15 minutes.

Form the dough into golf-ball-sized dumplings, then roll the dumplings in the extra flour to coat.

In a large saucepan over medium heat, bring the chicken stock to a simmer, add the dumplings and simmer on very gentle heat for 30–45 minutes until cooked through.

To serve, ladle the dumplings and broth into bowls, drizzle with extra virgin olive oil or truffle oil and garnish with grated Parmigiano-Reggiano.

DAD'S BEETROOT TARTS

These are made like tartes Tatin, but savoury instead of sweet. You could use a quality store-bought pastry made with butter, but homemade is worth the effort. You'll need 10cm-diameter frying-pans as the pans go straight from the stovetop into the oven. The secret is the addition of Pukara Estate Caramelised Balsamic Vinegar. With feta cheese and Pinoli pine nuts from Blenheim it's a divine combination.

Serves 6

9 canned cipollini onions in balsamic vinegar, sliced in half

180ml cipollini onion juice

3 baby red and 3 baby gold beetroots, cooked, peeled and each cut into 6 (see below)

6 x 10cm puff pastry rounds (storebought or see recipe below)

flour for dusting

130g soft feta

1 tbsp toasted Pinoli pine nuts

12 pea tendrils

Beetroot

6 baby beetroots (3 red and 3 gold)

100ml Pukara Estate Caramelised Balsamic Vinegar

Homemade Puff Pastry

250g strong plain flour

1 tsp fine sea salt

250g butter, cut into cubes, at room temperature, but not soft

100ml cold water

Preheat the oven to 180°C.

In each of 6 blini or 10cm-diameter pans, place 3 onion halves, 30ml onion juice, and 3 red and 3 gold pieces of beetroot. Bring to the boil over moderate heat and simmer to reduce the liquid by half. Remove from the heat, place a pastry round on top of the mixture in each pan and, using a teaspoon dusted in flour, pat the sides down around the edges, almost like an upside-down pie. Place in the oven and bake for 25 minutes. Remove from the oven and turn onto serving plates. Garnish each tart with 1½ tablespoons of feta, a sprinkle of pine nuts and 2 pea tendrils.

BEETROOT

Wash the beetroot and trim the roots and tops. Place in a saucepan, cover with cold salted water, bring to a simmer and cook until tender (about 10–12 minutes). Drain, cover with fresh cold water and leave to cool. When cool, rub the skins off while submerged under water. Slice each into 6 wedges and drizzle liberally with the balsamic vinegar.

HOMEMADE PUFF PASTRY

Sift the flour and salt into a large bowl. Add the butter to the bowl and rub it in loosely (small chunks of butter should be visible). Make a well in the flour, pour in the water, then mix to a firm, rough dough. Cover with plastic wrap and rest the dough for 20 minutes in the refrigerator.

Turn out onto a lightly floured surface, knead gently and form into a smooth rectangle. Roll the dough, in one direction only, until its length is 3 times its width, about 20 x 50cm. Keep edges straight and even. Don't overwork the butter streaks; you should have a marbled effect.

Fold into thirds. Give the dough a quarter turn and roll out again to 3 times its width. Fold as before, cover with plastic wrap and chill for at least 20 minutes. On a lightly floured surface roll out the pastry to a thickness of 5mm then cut out 6 x 10cm discs. Set aside until needed.

WHITEBAIT FRITTERS

It's worth investing in a small non-stick frying-pan to make these. The Gault secret is one egg to every 100g of whitebait. The egg just holds the whitebait together so you get a fritter that's packed full of whitebait. What's not to like about that?

Serves 4

4 eggs

4 pinches of nutmeg

4 tbsp fresh cream

4 pinches of salt

4 pinches of white pepper

400g whitebait

4 tsp butter

Lemon Parsley Mayo

4 tsp chopped curly parsley

½ cup mayonnaise

juice of 1 lemon

4 lemon wedges

Preheat the oven to 180°C.

In each of 4 cups place 1 egg, 1 pinch of nutmeg, 1 tablespoon cream and a pinch of salt and white pepper. Mix together with a fork. Add 100g of whitebait to each.

In a 10cm frying-pan, melt a teaspoon of butter, pour in one portion of whitebait mixture and cook on medium heat until golden, then turn and place the pan in the oven until the fritter is cooked through (6–8 minutes). Repeat with the remaining mixture.

Turn the cooked fritters onto a plate and serve with a sprig of parsley, a wedge of lemon and the Lemon Parsley Mayo alongside.

LEMON PARSLEY MAYO

In a bowl mix together the parsley, mayonnaise and lemon juice.

FAUX WHITEBAIT FRITTERS WITH TOMATO AND OLIVE SALAD

Here's something for vegetarians who don't eat whitebait – or for anyone who's squeamish about eating the real thing. Finely sliced silverbeet stems take the place of the whitebait. Celery salt is the crucial ingredient, so don't be tempted to leave it out. Leftover celery salt will make an excellent addition to a Bloody Mary.

Serves 2

1 egg, beaten

½ cup milk

3 tbsp flour

pinch of nutmeg

¼ tsp celery salt

pinch of white pepper

90g steamed silverbeet stems, finely sliced

2 tsp butter

2 sprigs chervil

Tomato and Olive Salad

4 tomatoes, roughly chopped

6 olives, pitted and roughly chopped

1 tsp marjoram

1 tsp extra virgin olive oil

1 tsp lemon juice

In a bowl, combine the egg, milk, flour and nutmeg to form a batter. Season with celery salt and white pepper. Allow to stand for 3 hours. Mix in the silverbeet stems. Melt 1 teaspoon of butter in a 10cm frying-pan, add half the mixture and fry until cooked through. Repeat with remaining mixture.

Place the fritters on plates, serve salad alongside and garnish with a sprig of chervil.

TOMATO AND OLIVE SALAD

For the salad, combine all the ingredients and season with salt and freshly ground black pepper.

ITALIAN BREAD SALAD

It is important to use top-quality anchovies in this salad. Spend a bit of money on buying the best, and even people who think they don't like anchovies will be delighted. My version of the classic Tuscan panzanella, this salad goes well with buffalo mozzarella served alongside.

Serves 4

10 vine-ripened tomatoes, seeded and roughly chopped

¼ small red onion, thinly sliced

1 cup roughly torn fresh basil

2 medium cloves garlic, minced

2 tbsp red wine vinegar

¼ cup extra virgin olive oil

1 tsp flaky salt

½ tsp freshly ground black pepper

1 tbsp capers (optional)

2 anchovy fillets, minced

2 cups torn stale ciabatta

Combine all the ingredients except the bread in a bowl.

Cover the bread with water and soak for 2–3 minutes until soft. Drain and squeeze out excess water.

Work the bread with your hands to break it up into popcorn-sized pieces. Mix the crumbled bread with the salad ingredients and serve.

Simon says

A tomato is fully ripe when it is dark red and has a uniform skin colour. It should be slightly soft and, most importantly, smell like a tomato.

MENU

a celebration dinner

This is the perfect menu to serve for a birthday dinner or some other special celebration. While the Duet of Carrot and Pea Soup calls for a little more preparation time and a steady hand, believe me, it is worth it, and my Crazy Chicken Kiev is so quick to prepare it more than makes up for it. My Molten Chocolate Puddings never fail to impress. You can make the mixture ahead of time, which is always a help when you're entertaining.

STARTER

Duet of Carrot and Pea Soup
(page 77)

MAIN

Crazy Chicken Kiev and Slaw
(page 92)

Bell House Potatoes
(page 169)

DESSERT

Simon Gault's Molten Chocolate Puddings
(page 191)

MUSHROOM SOUP

Mushrooms and sherry make a winning flavour combo and Tio Pepe sherry is the secret ingredient in this soup, although any dry sherry of your choice will work just fine. I've used button mushrooms, but use fresh field mushrooms if you're lucky enough to have some. What more can I say other than this soup is a real winner.

Serves 6

50ml olive oil

1 large onion, finely chopped

1kg button or field mushrooms, sliced

100g potatoes, peeled and sliced

1 litre vegetable stock

1 litre cream

50ml Tio Pepe sherry

1 tbsp finely chopped curly parsley to garnish

In a heavy-based saucepan heat the oil, add the onion and sauté without colouring until soft. Add the mushrooms and cook until there is no more liquid in the pan. Set aside.

In a separate saucepan place potatoes and stock, bring to the boil and simmer until the potato is cooked. Add this to the mushrooms and simmer for 5 minutes. Add the cream and sherry and return to the boil, then remove from the heat, place in a blender and purée. Pass through a sieve and return to the saucepan, bring to the boil and season to taste with salt and freshly ground black pepper. Pour into soup bowls, garnish with parsley and serve.

VENETIAN-STYLE PRAWNS

In this classic Venetian-style dish vinegar, onion, pine nuts and raisins give a wonderful sweet-and-sour flavour. This can be served slightly warm or at room temperature, which makes it an ideal dish to prepare before guests arrive. Blue cod also works well in place of prawns.

Serves 6

⅓ cup raisins

½ cup olive oil

2 large onions, thinly sliced

110ml white wine vinegar

1 tbsp sugar

⅓ cup fresh toasted pine nuts

24 prawn cutlets, peeled

½ cup flour

1 tbsp finely chopped curly parsley

Soak the raisins in warm water for 20 minutes, then drain. Set aside.

Meanwhile, heat ¼ cup of the oil in a medium frying-pan. Add the onions and sauté over medium heat until transparent. Increase the heat, add the vinegar, bring to the boil and cook for about 1 minute, stirring constantly, then add the sugar, pine nuts and reserved raisins. Cook for a further minute, then set aside.

Dust the prawn cutlets in flour. Heat the remaining oil in a large frying-pan, add the prawns, and fry over medium heat for 2–3 minutes on each side until golden. Drain on paper towels and season with salt.

Bring the onion sauce back to a simmer. Arrange the prawns in a single layer in a large shallow dish, spoon on the onion sauce and sprinkle with parsley. Cover the dish and allow to rest for at least 10 minutes. Spoon the prawns onto plates to serve, ideally at room temperature.

MUM'S VOODOO SANDWICHES

Who would have thought onion sandwiches could be such crowd-pleasers? Whenever a special occasion calls for finger food, Mum makes these, and they are sure to disappear pretty fast. The secret is to marinate the onions overnight in sugar syrup, which lightly pickles the onions.

Serves 8

2 medium onions

1 cup water

½ cup sugar

1 cup mayonnaise

½ tsp dry mustard powder

1 tsp lemon juice

1 loaf sliced sandwich bread

The day before required, thinly slice the onions into rings and place in a deep bowl. Combine the water and sugar in a saucepan, bring to the boil then pour onto the onion rings. Immediately cover the surface of the onions with ice cubes and place in the refrigerator.

In a bowl mix the mayonnaise, mustard and lemon juice. Refrigerate until required.

The next day, drain the onion rings and dry on paper towels.

Spread the mayonnaise mix on the number of bread slices required and top with onion rings. Season with salt and freshly ground black pepper and top each with another slice spread with the mayonnaise. Trim off the crusts and cut into triangles. Store in the refrigerator if not required immediately, or beneath a cool, damp tea towel.

Simon says
Refrigerate onions before chopping them to reduce the tears. Rubbing your hands with vinegar before and after slicing onions will eliminate any lingering smell.

VEGETABLE CLAFOUTIS

This recipe takes all the bits and pieces that are lying around in the fridge and transforms them into a fabulous dish that'll appeal to your vegetarian friends. Clafoutis is a French dessert from the region of Limousin consisting of seasonal fruit that is covered with batter and baked; however, this vegetable version makes a wonderful brunch item.

Serves 4

3 tbsp butter

2 leeks (white and light green part only), thoroughly cleaned and sliced

1 red capsicum, cored and diced

1 courgette, diced

4 whole eggs

2 egg yolks

3 tbsp flour

½ cup freshly grated Parmigiano-Reggiano, plus extra for topping

90ml milk

⅔ cup cream

⅓ cup chopped curly parsley

pinch of freshly grated nutmeg

6 large cherry tomatoes, thinly sliced into rounds

Preheat oven to 180°C.

In a frying-pan over medium heat melt 2 tablespoons of the butter, add the leeks and sauté until soft (about 3 minutes). Raise the heat and add the capsicum and courgette and cook for about 6 minutes. Set aside.

Meanwhile, in a bowl combine the eggs, yolks, flour, Parmigiano-Reggiano, milk, cream and parsley. Season with salt and pepper and nutmeg and whisk to combine.

Distribute the sautéed vegetables among 4 small buttered baking dishes. Pour the egg mixture over each portion. Scatter the tomato slices over the battered vegetables, sprinkle with extra Parmigiano-Reggiano and bake in the oven until cooked through and slightly golden on top (about 20 minutes).

Serve warm. You could also bake this in one large dish and cut into wedges to serve.

Simon says

Leftover egg whites can be frozen for later use. Pour them into a freezer container and seal tightly then label the container with the date and the number of egg whites. Defrost when ready to use. When whipping add a pinch of salt, as this helps to add volume to older egg whites.

MENU
buffet brunch

Sunday brunch is a relaxing way to entertain. Here I've suggested a selection of lighter dishes that can be served buffet-style with a glass or two of champagne. For dessert try Treacle Tarts served with coffee.

Cucumber and Chicken Liver Pâté Roulade
(page 45)

Parmesan Profiteroles
(page 40)

Kumara-Stuffed Tomatoes
(page 173)

Vegetable Clafoutis
(page 70)

DESSERT

Treacle Tarts
(page 206)

GREEN PEA SOUP

Everyone has a bag of frozen peas in their freezer, so this is a perfect anytime soup to make. The secret is not to cook the peas for too long – no longer than 10 minutes – so they retain their lovely bright green colour. For the same reason, when reheating the soup bring it just to the boil before serving. Don't be tempted to skimp on the cream – this gives the soup its wonderful velvety texture. I also like to drizzle a little truffle oil over. And for something a bit different, serving it in an espresso cup always looks flash.

Serves 6

50ml olive oil

1 medium onion, finely chopped

3 medium cloves garlic, finely chopped

1 cup cream

1 cup whole milk

1 litre chicken or vegetable stock

600g frozen baby peas

truffle oil to garnish

Heat the olive oil in a saucepan until shimmering (see note below), then add the onion and garlic and sauté until the onion is transparent, without burning the garlic. Add the cream, milk and stock, bring to the boil and then add the peas and gently simmer for 10 minutes.

Transfer the soup to a blender and process until smooth. Pass through a sieve and season with salt and white pepper.

Pour into 6 bowls and garnish with a swirl of truffle oil.

Simon says
'Shimmering' means the oil is heated to a point where the surface begins to ripple but does not smoke.

CARROT SOUP

Orange zest gives this soup its zing; butter and cream add richness. For something a bit novel, try serving the soup in small preserving jars.

Serves 6

50ml olive oil

1 medium onion, thinly sliced

2 medium cloves garlic, finely chopped

900g carrots, thinly sliced

1 tsp grated orange zest

1.35 litres chicken or vegetable stock

40g butter

300ml cream

2 tbsp crème fraîche

grated zest of ¼ orange

2 tbsp finely chopped chives

In a saucepan heat the olive oil until shimmering (see note page 74), then add the onion and garlic and sauté over medium heat for 3–6 minutes until the onion is transparent.

Add the carrots, orange zest and stock, bring to the boil then simmer for 30 minutes. Remove from the heat, transfer to a blender and purée until smooth. Return the soup to the saucepan and add the butter and cream. Bring back to the boil and simmer for 3 minutes. Season with salt and white pepper to your taste. Divide equally among 6 soup bowls, add a teaspoon of crème fraîche to each serve, top with orange zest and a pinch of salt and sprinkle with chopped chives.

DUET OF CARROT AND PEA SOUP

For something that looks really impressive, serve a bowl of my Carrot Soup and Green Pea Soup combined together.

Serves 12

1 quantity Carrot Soup (above)

1 quantity Green Pea Soup (page 74)

truffle oil to garnish

Make the Carrot Soup and the Green Pea Soup (see page 74), and ladle each into 2 separate jugs. Pour each soup in a slow, steady stream into opposite sides of each serving bowl, taking care that the soups do not combine. A drizzle of truffle oil over each serving adds the X factor.

mains

CHICKEN DRUMSTICKS WITH LEMON CAPER SAUCE AND SPAGHETTI

If there's just one recipe you cook from this book, this should be it. Packed with flavour, it is a cinch to make. The spaghetti is a winner, even on its own, or try it with prawns or smoked chicken. Fantastic!

Serves 4

1 cup flour

8 free-range chicken drumsticks

4 tbsp extra virgin olive oil

2 tbsp butter

1 lemon, thinly sliced

4 cloves garlic, minced

20 pitted green olives, roughly sliced

¼ cup capers

½ cup white wine

1 cup chicken stock

Spaghetti

450g spaghetti

120ml extra virgin olive oil

2 cloves garlic, minced

½ small red chilli, finely chopped (seeds optional)

½ tsp salt

2 tbsp butter

4 tbsp finely chopped parsley

Parmigiano-Reggiano for garnish (optional)

Preheat the oven to 180°C.

Place the flour in a plastic bag, add the chicken and toss to coat evenly. Remove from the bag and shake off any excess flour.

In a heavy casserole dish over medium heat, place the olive oil and butter. When the butter is foaming, add the drumsticks and brown for 3 minutes on each side. Add the lemon, garlic, olives, capers, wine and stock, bring to the boil and then transfer the dish to the oven and cook for 30 minutes until the chicken is ready to fall from the bone. Keep warm.

Bring a large saucepan of lightly salted water to the boil, add the spaghetti and cook until just al dente. Drain.

In a separate pan, heat the oil and sauté the garlic and chilli until the garlic just begins to brown, then add the salt. Remove from the heat and add the drained spaghetti, then stir in the butter and parsley. Divide the spaghetti between the serving plates and top with the chicken and sauce. Grate over the Parmigiano-Reggiano and add a grind of black pepper if desired.

OYSTER-STUFFED CHICKEN

Roast chicken is a great standard and here's a way to jazz it up. This is one of those old-school dishes that my mum used to make. If you've got someone coming to dinner who loves oysters, it's a sure way to impress.

Serves 6

450g oysters with the juice

1 green capsicum, cored and chopped

3 tbsp finely chopped celery

6 tbsp chopped curly parsley

½ onion, chopped

4 cloves garlic, crushed

zest of 1 lemon

90g butter

1 tsp cayenne pepper

1 cup fresh breadcrumbs

3 x size 11 chickens, cut in half (through breastbone from inside the cavity, then along backbone)

1 tsp salt

½ cup water

3 lemons, halved

flat-leaf parsley sprigs to garnish

Preheat the oven to 190°C. Drain and chop the oysters, reserving their liquor. Sauté the oysters, capsicum, celery, parsley, onion, garlic and lemon zest in 60g of the butter for 10 minutes, then add the cayenne pepper, breadcrumbs and ½ cup of oyster liquor. Combine and set aside.

Meanwhile, place the chickens in a shallow roasting pan skin-side up, dot with the remaining butter and season with the salt and some freshly ground black pepper. Add the water to the pan. Roast in the oven for 20 minutes or until brown.

Remove the chickens from the oven, turn skin-side down and fill each cavity with oyster stuffing. Roast for a further 20 minutes or until golden brown and the stuffing is crunchy (turn on the grill for the last few minutes if necessary). Serve with lemon halves and garnish with flat-leaf parsley.

Simon says

For best results, cook chicken at 190°C, allowing 45 minutes per kilogram plus a further 20 minutes. For the best flavour it is worth paying a little more for organic, free-range or corn-fed chicken. The flesh will be less spongy, as a bird that has been allowed to forage free will have built up muscle tone.

SAGE AND PARMESAN PORK SCHNITZEL

There's something about the crisp coating that makes schnitzel a real crowd-pleaser. Parmesan and sage give the crust on my version the wow factor. I've used pork here, but the crumb coating would be just as good on chicken. Serve it with mash for a dish just like Mum made, only better.

Serves 4

1 cup flour

3 eggs, beaten

1 cup panko crumbs

12 large sage leaves, finely chopped, plus 4 sprigs extra

½ cup grated Parmigiano-Reggiano

4 pork schnitzels

8 tbsp olive oil

4 tbsp butter

1 lemon, quartered

Place the flour in a shallow dish and season with salt and freshly ground black pepper. Place the eggs in another shallow dish. Place the panko crumbs, sage and Parmigiano in a third shallow dish. Coat the schnitzels with flour, dip in the egg, then coat with crumb mixture. Allow to stand for 5 minutes.

Cook the schnitzels one at time. In a large frying-pan, heat 1 tablespoon of oil until shimmering (see note page 74), then add 1 tablespoon of butter. Just as the butter is melting, add a schnitzel and fry for 2 minutes on each side or until browned. Remove and keep warm while repeating with the remaining schnitzels.

Just before serving, in a small frying-pan heat the remaining 4 tablespoons of olive oil until shimmering and fry the whole sage leaves for a few seconds until crisp.

Serve the schnitzels with my Mashed Potato (see page 114) and garnished with fried sage leaves and with lemon quarters alongside.

Simon says
Freeze the rinds of hard cheese such as Parmigiano-Reggiano and use them to enrich the flavour of any soup. Toss them into the pot, simmer, and remove before serving.

HONEYED FISH FILLETS

Ginger, honey and orange juice – what a wonderful combination. Add some mustard and soy sauce, and it's sheer magic. The flour on the fish is the secret, as it absorbs the sauce. This is a fancy-pants fish dish that's really quick and easy to prepare.

Serves 2

1 tsp freshly grated ginger

4 tbsp bush honey

75ml fresh orange juice

1 tsp hot mustard

1 tbsp zested orange peel

3 shallots, thinly sliced

1 tsp soy sauce
(or teriyaki sauce)

¼ tsp chilli powder

2 x 200g skinned and
boned firm fish fillets
(I've used snapper)

2 tbsp flour

2 tbsp olive oil

2 tbsp butter

1 bunch bok choy, trimmed and
leaves separated

fish sauce for seasoning
(optional)

Combine the first 8 ingredients in a saucepan, heat to a simmer, then simmer for 4 minutes.

Season the fish fillets with salt and black pepper, then lightly dust with flour. Heat 1 tablespoon of the olive oil in a frying-pan over medium heat until it shimmers (see note page 74). Place 1 tablespoon of butter in the pan, and as the butter starts to melt place a fish fillet, skin-side up, on top. Fry for about 3 minutes each side until cooked. Repeat with the other fillet.

Place the fillets on plates and pour the sauce over. Serve with steamed bok choy, seasoned with fish sauce if desired.

SAVOURY PORK CHOPS WITH APPLE AND SAGE CRUMBLE

Here the pork chops are cooked with a crumble topping that includes apple and fresh sage – always a winning combination with pork. Serve with my Broccoli with Lemon Dill Dressing.

Serves 6

Savoury Pork Chops

6 pork loin chips

3 tbsp extra virgin olive oil

4 Granny Smith apples, peeled, quartered and cored

1 onion, finely chopped

100ml water

120g fresh breadcrumbs

8 large sage leaves, chopped

lemon wedges to serve

Lemon Dill Dressing

90ml extra virgin olive oil

2 tbsp lemon juice

grated zest of 1 lemon

¼ tsp freshly ground black pepper

3 tsp chopped fresh dill

salt to taste

1 large head broccoli

Preheat the oven to 190°C. Season the chops and fry gently in the olive oil on each side to brown and partly cook. Place in a small baking dish.

Meanwhile, place the apples, onion and water in a saucepan and simmer until tender. Mash well together with the breadcrumbs and sage and season with salt and pepper. Spread the stuffing mixture on top of the chops and bake in the oven for 12–13 minutes until the crumble browns and the pork is cooked through. Serve with the broccoli (recipe follows) and lemon wedges on the side.

STEAMED BROCCOLI WITH LEMON DILL DRESSING

Combine all the ingredients except the broccoli in a bowl and mix with a whisk.

Trim the stems from the broccoli. Wash and peel the stems and then cut into strips (as shown in photograph). Cut the florets into small, uniform pieces and set aside.

Bring a large saucepan of water to the boil. Add the broccoli stems and boil for 1 minute. Add the florets and boil for a further 2 minutes. Drain and rinse under cold running water. Drain again. Place in a large bowl and gently toss with the dressing. Serve immediately.

CRAYFISH THERMIDOR

One of those dishes guaranteed to impress guests, this is a celebratory meal that looks fantastic on the plate if you fan out the crayfish legs. The béarnaise sauce is also a wonderful accompaniment to eye fillet. Don't be frightened of making béarnaise – the key is to keep it warm until you are ready to serve; otherwise the butter will set.

Serves 6

3 x 500g live crayfish

4 egg yolks

4 tbsp vinegar reduction (see below)

250ml clarified butter, warmed

2 tomatoes, seeded and diced

4 tbsp freshly chopped tarragon

4 tbsp freshly chopped parsley

40g Parmigiano-Reggiano, grated

1 tbsp Dijon mustard

Vinegar Reduction

100ml white wine

100ml white wine vinegar

1 shallot, finely sliced

2 sprigs tarragon

1 bay leaf

1 sprig thyme

3 black peppercorns

See page 231 for instructions on how to prepare crayfish for cooking. Bring a large saucepan of water to the boil over high heat, then place the crayfish in and quickly bring back to the boil. Cook for 1 minute per 100g (5 minutes here). As soon as the time is up, plunge the crayfish into iced water and leave to cool completely (about 30 minutes). When cool, cut in half lengthwise and quickly rinse under cold running water, being sure to remove the brain and the black tube running down the tail. Cover and refrigerate.

To make the vinegar reduction, place the wine, vinegar, shallot, herbs and peppercorns in a saucepan, bring to the boil and simmer to reduce by half, then pass through a fine strainer and leave to cool.

For the béarnaise, place the egg yolks in a stainless steel bowl (or top of a double-boiler) with 4 tablespoons of vinegar reduction, place over a saucepan of boiling water and whisk until the mixture coats the back of a spoon to form a sabayon. Be very careful not to scramble the egg (this gives the béarnaise an overpowering egg flavour). You may have to take the bowl off the heat a few times if you think it is getting too hot. As soon as the sabayon has thickened, remove from the heat and slowly pour in the clarified butter, whisking continuously until incorporated.

Remove the crayfish meat from the shells and slice into neat bite-sized pieces, place in a bowl, and add the chopped tomato, tarragon, parsley, Parmigiano-Reggiano and mustard. Add enough of the béarnaise to coat the mixture generously, then gently mix to combine everything (if you mix too hard, the crayfish will break down). Season with salt and freshly ground black pepper.

Preheat the oven grill. Place the crayfish shells on an oven tray and spoon the crayfish mixture carefully into the shells, making sure there is an even amount of mixture throughout each; don't forget to fill the head cavity, too.

Place under the grill and cook for 7–10 minutes or until golden brown and hot on the inside. Place on plates, fan out the legs and serve.

CRAZY CHICKEN KIEV AND SLAW

Chicken Kiev was a dish that featured on pretty much every restaurant menu in the 1980s. My contemporary version is stuffed with soft goat's cheese, which becomes lovely and creamy when the chicken is cooked. A nutty coating made from macadamia nuts and flavoured with Parmigiano-Reggiano and Cajun spice replaces the more traditional breadcrumb crust. I like to serve it with a crunchy slaw, which would also be great with my Sage and Parmesan Pork Schnitzel (see page 84).

Serves 4

200g soft goat's cheese

grated zest of 1 lemon

2 cloves garlic, finely chopped

4 skinless chicken breasts

16 large basil leaves

2 eggs, lightly beaten

1 tbsp Dijon mustard

1 cup flour

½ cup grated Parmigiano-Reggiano

½ cup crushed macadamia nuts

1 tbsp Cajun spice (available at supermarkets)

500ml canola oil

Preheat the oven to 180°C.

In a small bowl, mix the goat's cheese, lemon zest and 1 clove of the garlic. Set aside.

Butterfly each breast, season with salt and freshly ground black pepper and place 4 basil leaves in a row on each breast, covering as much of the surface as possible. Divide the cheese mixture into 4 equal amounts and spoon onto the breasts. Roll the breasts to enclose the filling. Season again.

In a bowl, mix the eggs, remaining garlic and mustard. Place the flour in another bowl, and in a third bowl combine the Parmigiano, nuts and Cajun spice. Season to taste.

Dip each breast in the flour and then the egg mixture, then coat thoroughly in the nut mixture, repeating if necessary.

Heat the oil in a large frying-pan until hot (around 170°C), add the chicken and shallow-fry for just a few seconds on each side until the crumb is golden. Place on a baking tray and bake in the oven for 15–20 minutes until cooked through. Serve the chicken with the slaw alongside.

Slaw

½ green cabbage, thinly sliced

¼ red cabbage, thinly sliced

1 cup mayonnaise

2 tbsp good-quality balsamic vinegar

SLAW

While the chicken is baking, in a bowl mix the cabbage, mayonnaise and balsamic, and season to taste. (Using good-quality balsamic vinegar makes all the difference here. See my 'five per cent magic ingredients', page 229.)

DAD'S SAGE CHICKEN

The sneaky part to this recipe is putting the sage under the skin of the chicken so it doesn't burn while the chicken cooks, whether in the oven or on a barbecue or grill. So simple, so good.

Serves 4

4 chicken legs

20 large sage leaves

1 clove garlic, peeled and thinly sliced

flaky salt to taste

1 tbsp butter

Preheat the oven to 185°C.

Using your fingers, gently separate the skin from each leg and place 4 leaves of sage under the skin on the top side of each leg and 1 leaf under the skin on the underside of each. Likewise, distribute the slices of garlic evenly under the skin of the legs. Season with salt and cracked black pepper, both under and over the skin.

Heat an ovenproof frying-pan or grill pan and melt the butter until it bubbles. Place the legs skin-side down in the pan, then place in the oven on the bottom shelf and cook for 25 minutes, turning once, until golden and cooked through, then serve.

Simon says

Always brush chicken with oil before grilling to prevent it sticking to the barbecue or hot plate.

MENU

a vegetarian dinner

Inviting vegetarian guests for dinner can be somewhat daunting, especially if you're cooking for meat-eaters as well. You don't want your vegetarian guests to feel that you've created the entire meal just for them or, worse, for your meat-eating guests to feel that something is missing from their plates. I promise that with this menu you'll keep everybody happy.

STARTER

Dad's Beetroot Tarts
(page 50)

MAIN

Pasta Soufflé
(page 112)

DESSERT

Fruit Salad Deluxe
(page 212)

BEEF STROGANOFF

Everyone of a certain age remembers eating Beef Stroganoff. There's a reason this kind of classic dish hangs around – because it tastes so damn good. The Marmite is something my grandmother used to add, which now seems odd – but it works. Cooked chicken could be substituted for the beef.

Serves 6

60g butter

900g sirloin steak, sliced into strips

1 large onion, finely chopped

1 clove garlic, finely chopped

230g fresh mushrooms, sliced

3 tbsp flour

2 tsp Marmite

1 tbsp tomato sauce

300ml beef stock

¼ cup dry white wine

240g sour cream

¼ tsp dried or chopped fresh dill, plus 6 sprigs fresh dill to garnish

Jasmine Rice (see page 178) to serve

Slowly heat a frying-pan, add 1 tablespoon of the butter and, when melted, add the meat and quickly sear on both sides. Remove the meat and set aside.

Place the remaining butter in the same pan, add the onion, garlic and mushrooms and sauté until soft, then set aside with the meat. Add the flour, Marmite and tomato sauce to the pan, and season to taste with salt and freshly ground black pepper. Stir until smooth, then gradually add the stock and wine, stirring constantly, and bring to the boil. Reduce the heat and simmer for 5 minutes over low heat. Add the sour cream and dill, and stir until well combined. Return the beef and vegetables to the pan and heat through.

Meanwhile, prepare Jasmine Rice according to the recipe on page 178. Leave the lid on to keep it warm. When ready to serve, fluff up the rice with a fork.

Divide the rice and stroganoff among 6 plates and garnish each with a sprig of dill.

YELLOWFIN TUNA AND BUFFALO MOZZARELLA SALAD

I included this dish on the first-ever menu at my restaurant Euro, and it's been there ever since. One of my most popular dishes, it relies on top-quality Italian buffalo mozzarella or bocconcini (or use the locally made bocconcini from Clevedon Valley Buffalo Company, the best mozzarella in the country). The secret to cooking tuna is to take it out of the refrigerator an hour before cooking so it reaches room temperature in the middle. Sear the tuna for 20 seconds only on each side; otherwise it will be dry.

Serves 6

70ml extra virgin olive oil

12 small vine-ripened tomatoes, halved

3 tbsp capers (if salted, soak in cold water)

24 fresh basil leaves, torn

36 fresh marjoram leaves, roughly torn

375g Italian buffalo mozzarella, cut into 18 pieces (or use whole bocconcini)

1 medium clove garlic, minced

juice of 2 lemons

900g yellowfin tuna, cut into 150g portions, at room temperature

In a bowl place 50ml of the olive oil, the tomatoes, capers, basil and marjoram. Add the mozzarella along with the garlic and lemon juice. Season with salt and cracked black pepper and gently combine. This can be done up to 3 hours in advance.

Remove the tuna from the refrigerator an hour before cooking. Coat the tuna pieces in the remaining olive oil, then place on the hot chargrill of the barbecue for 20 seconds each side. Remove, slice in half and season.

Divide the tuna and salad equally among the plates, then pour the juice that has accumulated in the bowl over the salad for dressing.

Simon says

To store tuna, remove packaging, rinse fish under cold water and pat dry with paper towels. Fish deteriorates when it sits in its own juices, so place it on a cake rack in a shallow pan filled with crushed ice. Cover with cling wrap or foil and set in the coldest part of the refrigerator. Tuna will keep well this way for up to 2 days.

ROSEMARY ROASTED PORK LOIN WITH HAZELNUTS

This is one of those dishes that shows how good simple cooking can be. The sauce is an absolute show-stopper. None of the cooking flavour is wasted, as the juices from the meat are added to the sauce. The addition of white wine is key, and make sure your hazelnuts are fresh. The secret weapon is a meat thermometer – it makes cooking meat so much easier.

Serves 4

2 tbsp very finely chopped rosemary leaves, plus 3 extra sprigs

2 medium cloves garlic, minced

2 tbsp extra virgin olive oil

1 boneless pork loin (around 1kg)

½ cup white wine

1 cup chicken or vegetable stock

½ cup hazelnuts, toasted and roughly chopped

2 tbsp butter

Preheat the oven to 200°C.

Combine the rosemary, garlic and olive oil and rub the mixture all over the pork loin. Season with salt and freshly ground black pepper. Place in a roasting pan and roast in the oven for 40 minutes or until an internal temperature of 63°C is reached.

Remove the roast from the oven, take the pork from the pan and set aside to rest so the juices redistribute through the meat.

Meanwhile, place the roasting pan on the stovetop and bring the pan juices to a simmer. Add the wine, stock and 2 sprigs of rosemary, then simmer until reduced by half. Add the hazelnuts and bring to the boil. Remove the rosemary and add the butter. When it is almost melted, turn off the heat and give the pan a quick shake to emulsify the sauce.

Slice the pork, place on a large platter and spoon the hazelnut sauce over and around the pork. Garnish with a sprig of rosemary.

MEATLESS CASSEROLE

One of my mum's favourites, this is ideal for a cheap, simple meal without meat; or it can also be served cold, cut in small pieces, as a savoury for lunch. It's not often served at my place, but I love cabbage and it gives this dish a great consistency.

Serves 2

1½ cups grated Cheddar, or your favourite cheese

2 level cups cooked rice (from 1 cup uncooked)

10 semidried tomatoes, roughly chopped

1 large onion, finely chopped and fried until transparent

1 level cup finely sliced cabbage

2 eggs, well beaten

2 tbsp flour

2 tbsp chopped curly parsley

Preheat the oven to 185°C. Reserve half the cheese and mix all the remaining ingredients except the parsley thoroughly, and season well with salt and freshly ground black pepper. Place in a greased casserole dish and sprinkle the top with the reserved cheese. Bake in the oven for 35 minutes until golden and the edges are crisp. Remove from the oven, sprinkle with chopped parsley and serve.

Simon says

To dry tomatoes, preheat the oven on its lowest setting – no more than 50°C. Halve the tomatoes and scoop out the seeds using your thumb. Place the tomatoes cut side up on a lined baking tray and lightly sprinkle with salt. Position the tray in the centre of the oven and prop the oven door open. (I do this with a wine cork which I place lengthwise between the top of the door and the door frame.) The drying time will be 8–10 hours depending on the thickness of the tomatoes. When they are ready, the skins will be shrivelled or puckered and the underside will look dry. Store in olive oil. These are delicious in a salad.

DAD'S STEAK AND KIDNEY PUDDING

This is my dad's recipe and it's a real show-off item made with a good old-fashioned suet pastry, which gives a delicious crust. So long as you get the thickness of the pastry right, it's fail-safe. Make it in a pudding bowl and turn it out for an impressive centrepiece.

Serves 6

Suet Pastry

2¼ cups self-raising flour

175g Shreddo (see page 233)

½ tsp salt

Filling

900g cross-cut blade steak

300g ox kidney

2 tbsp flour

2 tsp salt

1 tsp freshly ground black pepper

1 large onion, diced

½ cup beef stock

Mix the flour, Shreddo and salt with enough water (about 1 cup) to form a soft, dryish dough. Knead on a floured surface until it comes together. Set aside about one-quarter for the lid. Roll out the remaining pastry to a round to line a greased (or non-stick) pudding basin (capacity 2.5–3 litres), with the edges slightly overhanging to seal the lid.

Dice the steak and kidney into 2.5cm cubes, discarding any gristle and fat from both.

Place the flour, salt and pepper in a plastic bag large enough to hold all the meat. Add the meat to the bag and close the opening, including as much air as possible, and shake well to coat the meat with the seasoned flour.

Combine the onion with the floured meat and spoon into the pastry-lined basin. Pour in the stock to cover two-thirds of the meat.

Roll out the reserved pastry to form the lid. Wet the lip of the pastry in the basin and cover with the pastry lid, sealing together by pressing with the tines of a fork. Cover the pudding with a clamp-on lid, or use greased aluminium foil or a pudding cloth, tying securely in place.

Quarter fill with water a saucepan large enough to hold the basin and bring to the boil. Lower in the basin, cover and steam for 6½ hours. Check from time to time and top up the saucepan with more boiling water if necessary. Turn the pudding out onto a serving dish and cut wedges to serve.

MUM'S LAMB SHANKS

This is my take on one of my mum's classic dishes. The list of ingredients is long, but this is one of those dishes that comes together with very little effort. And it tastes fantastic. You'll know the lamb shanks are cooked when the meat is starting to fall off the bone. If it's not at that point, it will be tough.

Serves 6

4 tbsp olive oil

6 lamb shanks

1 onion, cut into 6 wedges

1 tsp ground cumin

½ tsp each Spanish smoked sweet paprika and ground ginger

3 carrots, coarsely chopped

1 quantity Red Capsicum Harissa (recipe below)

2 tbsp tomato paste

2 tsp flaky salt

1 red and 1 yellow capsicum, cored and cut into wide strips

400g can chickpeas, drained

150g peas, fresh or frozen

4 tbsp each chopped flat-leaf parsley and coriander leaves

3 cups chicken stock

3 cups couscous

300ml veal jus (available at the supermarket), heated

Red Capsicum Harissa

1 red capsicum, halved and cored

4–5 fresh, long red chillies (about 100g)

2 tsp each ground cumin and ground coriander

1 clove garlic, peeled

1 tsp salt

½ cup olive oil

Heat 2 tablespoons of the olive oil in a large saucepan with a lid and brown the lamb shanks in batches over high heat. Add the onion, cumin, smoked paprika and ginger then return all the lamb to the pan, along with the carrots, ¼ cup harissa (reserve the rest for serving) and tomato paste. Cover with cold water, add the salt and bring to the boil, then reduce the heat and simmer, covered, for 50 minutes.

Add the capsicum and chickpeas and cook for a further 40 minutes, then add the peas and cook for a further 5 minutes or until the meat is very tender and almost falling off the bone. (You may need to add more stock if the level drops below the lamb shanks.) Stir in half the parsley and coriander, and season to taste.

Bring the chicken stock and 2 tablespoons of olive oil to the boil and pour the stock over the couscous. Cover with plastic wrap and let stand until at room temperature. Use a fork to loosen the grains. Add the remaining parsley and coriander, and season to taste.

To serve, spoon couscous into the centre of the plates, place the vegetables around the couscous, top each serving of couscous with a lamb shank, then pour 50ml of the heated veal jus over each serving. Serve the warmed harissa in a jug on the side.

RED CAPSICUM HARISSA

Makes about 1½ cups

Preheat the oven to 200°C. Roast the capsicum halves in the oven skin-side up until thoroughly cooked (about 12 minutes). Place in a plastic bag, seal and leave for 20 minutes. Remove the capsicum from the bag, peel and roughly chop.

Place the chillies on a foil-lined oven tray and grill under high heat for 8–10 minutes, turning occasionally, until the skin blisters and blackens. Place in a plastic bag to cool, then peel and seed. Combine the chilli, capsicum, cumin, ground coriander, garlic and salt in a blender and process until finely chopped. Add olive oil in a thin steady stream, while blending, to form a smooth sauce.

Harissa will keep for 2 weeks in an airtight container in the refrigerator.

PASTA SOUFFLÉ

This is really just a fancy macaroni cheese, using Parmigiano-Reggiano, the king of Italian cheeses. For a nice vegetarian meal, serve it with some rocket salad on the side tossed with balsamic vinegar, olive oil, shaved Manchego cheese and pine nuts.

Serves 8–10

160g butter

¾ cup flour

4 cups hot milk

½ tsp freshly grated nutmeg

1 cup freshly grated Emmental

¾ cup freshly grated Parmigiano-Reggiano

4 egg yolks

450g tagliatelle pasta, fresh or dried

8 egg whites

1 tomato, sliced into rounds

flaky salt to taste

Preheat the oven to 180°C. Bring a large saucepan of salted water to the boil. Meanwhile, butter a deep, straight-sided baking dish or six 400ml soufflé ramekins with 1 tablespoon of the butter, then set aside.

Melt 100g of butter in a medium saucepan over medium-low heat. Whisk in the flour and cook until golden brown (about 5 minutes). Remove from the heat and gradually whisk in the milk (very slowly at first so no lumps form), then return the pan to medium-low heat and cook the béchamel, whisking constantly, until slightly thickened (about 15 minutes). Add nutmeg and season generously with salt and freshly ground white pepper. Remove the pan from the heat, whisk in the grated cheeses and set aside to cool slightly.

Add the egg yolks to the sauce one at a time, stirring well after each addition. Set aside to cool, stirring often.

Blanch the pasta in boiling salted water for 1 minute for fresh pasta, or 3 minutes if dried. Reserve 5 tablespoons of the cooking water in a large bowl, then drain the pasta and add to the bowl. Add the remaining butter and toss well. Add the sauce and toss well, then taste and adjust seasoning.

Beat the egg whites in a large bowl until firm peaks form, then fold into the pasta mixture in 2 batches. Transfer to the prepared dish or ramekins and top with tomato slices.

Bake for 40 minutes until puffed and golden. Serve immediately.

APRICOT, DATE & WALNUT CHICKEN CASSEROLE

Everybody has a favourite chicken casserole. This is mine. It's super-easy to make – all you have to do is place all the ingredients in a casserole dish, and an hour later you have something that tastes incredible. This goes well with my Mashed Potato.

Serves 4

1 x 1.2kg chicken, cut into 8 pieces

4 tbsp flour

4 tbsp olive oil

1 large onion, finely chopped

6 dried apricots, cut into slivers

6 dried or fresh dates, roughly chopped

12 walnuts

2 sprigs marjoram

300ml white wine

2 tbsp wholegrain mustard

800ml water

zest of 1 orange

Mashed Potato

2kg Agria potatoes, peeled and chopped

100g butter, cubed

½ cup milk, hot

½ cup cream, hot

pinch of nutmeg

2 tbsp chopped parsley or chives

Preheat the oven to 185°C. Season the chicken pieces with salt and freshly ground black pepper, then place in a plastic bag with the flour, seal and shake to coat.

Heat the olive oil until hot in a casserole dish. Remove the chicken pieces from the bag and sauté in the oil until golden brown. Add the remaining ingredients, grating the zest of half the orange into the dish. Cover and place in the oven for 1 hour.

Remove from the oven and, using a zester or microplane, zest the remaining orange peel over the top to garnish. Serve with Mashed Potato.

MASHED POTATO

In a saucepan, cover the potatoes with cold salted water and bring to the boil. Simmer until just past tender. Drain and pass through a potato ricer or mash with a potato masher.

Combine the butter and hot milk and cream. Return the mashed potato to the heat, add the milk mixture and stir until smooth and creamy (you may not need all the liquid, depending on how starchy the potatoes are). Add the nutmeg and herbs and season with salt and freshly ground black pepper to taste.

Simon says
Don't overbeat the potatoes, or you will end up with a starchy, sticky mash.

ROAST DUCK WITH CHERRY SAUCE

When I was an apprentice at Antoine's restaurant in Auckland, my job every day was to cook the duck and orange sauce. This is my adaptation of the classic dish, Duck à l'Orange, in which I've used cherries. Frozen cherries work just as well as fresh ones, so it's something that you can cook all year round.

Serves 4

½ cup sugar

80ml water

20ml triple sec

60ml crème de cassis

250ml orange juice, strained

1 tbsp cornflour

100g pitted cherries, minced

50g pitted cherries, roughly chopped

2 x size 22 ducks (head and feet removed)

For the sauce, make a caramel by placing the sugar and water in a saucepan and bringing to the boil. Do not stir, but swirl the pan if necessary, brushing the sides with a wet pastry brush a few times to prevent any sugar crystals forming and burning. Allow the mixture to simmer until beginning to turn the colour of caramel. Just before this stage is reached, remove from the heat and carefully add the triple sec (be careful not to burn yourself while doing this). Pour in the crème de cassis and orange juice, then bring back to a simmer for 15 minutes.

Combine the cornflour with 2 tablespoons of water to a smooth, runny paste and whisk it into the sauce. Add the minced and chopped cherries and bring the sauce back to the boil. Set aside. (The sauce can be made in advance and stored in an airtight container in the refrigerator for up to a month.)

Preheat the oven to 160°C. Using a boning knife, remove the wishbones from the ducks (this makes it easier to halve them later). Trim off excess fat. Season the entire skin of each bird with salt and freshly ground black pepper and place in a roasting pan. Place in the oven for 90 minutes or until the internal temperature reaches 72°C.

Remove the ducks from the oven and set aside in a warm place for 20 minutes. Cut the ducks in half lengthwise on either side of the backbone, and discard the backbone. Reheat the sauce, then place the half ducks on platters, pour the sauce over and serve.

MENU

midwinter dinner

My mum's Lamb Shanks and my grandmother's Golden Syrup Pudding are just the thing for a hearty midwinter meal. The lamb shanks cook long and slow, so the house will be filled with the wonderful aroma of them cooking in the oven when your guests arrive. With the main dish and dessert taken care of in advance, all that's left to do is prepare the Shrimp Fritters as guests arrive.

STARTER

Shrimp Fritters
(page 18)

MAIN

Mum's Lamb Shanks
(page 111)

DESSERT

Golden Syrup Pudding
(page 192)

HAPUKU IN A BAG

Cooking food in a bag, or *en papillote*, is a very old French technique that cooks the food in its own juices to intensify the flavour. I like to serve the parcels intact so guests can open them up themselves. Horseradish and smoked paprika may seem a slightly unusual combo, but they work really well together. I would serve this as a course on its own, maybe preceded by a substantial starter such as the Bread Dumplings and Tomatoes (see page 37).

Serves 2

2 tbsp butter

2 x 200g hapuku steaks
(or other firm, thick white fish)

2 tsp horseradish cream

2 slices lemon, skin on

6 olives, pitted and halved

8 capers

2 tbsp peeled, seeded and finely
diced tomato

4 pinches of Spanish
smoked paprika

2 large raw prawns,
peeled and deveined

2 sprigs chervil

2 tbsp extra virgin olive oil

2 tbsp white balsamic vinegar

Preheat the oven to 180°C. Place 2 x 30cm squares of baking paper on a flat surface. Place ½ tablespoon of butter on each square, then place a hapuku steak directly on top. Spread half the horseradish over each, then top each with a slice of lemon, 3 olives, 4 capers, half the tomato and another ½ tablespoon of butter, then dust with the smoked paprika. Finally, place a prawn neatly on each portion and top with a sprig of chervil.

To seal the bags, lift up the sides along the length of the fish and pinch and fold together from each corner, forming a cup shape and ensuring they are tightly sealed. Before completely sealing the bag pour half the oil and half the vinegar into each, then seal by folding and pinching along the top.

Place both bags on a baking tray and into the oven for 10 minutes or until the fish is just cooked through.

Serve the bags on plates to open at the table.

Simon says

Capers add salt and peppery flavours to a dish, so it may not need seasoning. Rinse capers before using to wash away any saltiness. If they are packed in salt, soak overnight. Capers are available in various sizes; the smaller they are the more intense the flavour, and I find salted capers are the best for quality and flavour.

SPANISH FRIED RICE

This is one dish you don't need to worry about overcooking. If you do, there will be a race to get the crunchy bits that form around the sides of the pan. A classic Spanish dish from Valencia, paella (also the Spanish name for the pan it's cooked in) is one of those dishes you can adapt according to taste. This is my mum's version. Feel free to add mussels, shrimps and scallops, or whatever selection takes your fancy. I would serve this dish in the middle of the table, so that everyone just tucks in.

Serves 4

4 tbsp olive oil

225g fresh fish, cut into chunks

1 onion, chopped

3 medium cloves garlic, finely chopped

1 red capsicum, cored, seeded and sliced

4 tomatoes, peeled and chopped

1¼ cups carnaroli rice

450ml fish stock

150ml white wine

¾ cup frozen peas

5 saffron threads, steeped in 2 tbsp hot water

150g cooked and peeled prawns

Heat 2 tablespoons of the olive oil in a paella pan or large frying-pan (you may need to use 2 frying-pans if you do not have one large enough). Add the fish to the pan, stir-fry for 2 minutes then transfer to a mixing bowl with all the juices and set aside.

Heat the remaining olive oil in the pan and add the onion, garlic and capsicum. Fry for 6–7 minutes, stirring frequently, until the onion and capsicum have softened.

Stir in the tomatoes, cook for a further 2 minutes, then add the rice, stirring to coat the grains, and cook for 2–3 minutes.

Pour in the stock and wine, then add the peas and saffron water, season well with salt and freshly ground black pepper and combine all the ingredients. Gently stir in the reserved fish along with all the juices, and the prawns. Cook over a gentle heat for 25 minutes or until the stock has been absorbed but the mixture is still moist.

Place under a grill for about 5 minutes to give the top of the rice some colour. Remove from the heat and leave to stand for 5 minutes before serving in the pan at the table.

COQ AU VIN ON RISOTTO

This chicken dish is one of those unbeatable French classics. I add brandy and chardonnay to my version. It's a dish that tastes really good on its own, but I like to serve it with risotto. The key to great risotto is not to let it get dry – it should have a creamy, almost fluid consistency when poured into a serving dish, which the Italians call *all'onda* (like a wave). Using the bacon from the chicken dish in the risotto gives it that five per cent magic. Start this dish a day ahead.

Serves 6

1 whole chicken
(size 16, or 1.6kg)

1 large onion, finely chopped

6 rashers rindless streaky bacon,
roughly chopped

4 cloves garlic, roughly chopped

1 sprig thyme

2 bay leaves

1½ cups chardonnay

200ml chicken stock

100ml brandy

2 tsp salt

½ tsp freshly ground
black pepper

300g button mushrooms, sliced

Risotto

3 tbsp extra virgin olive oil

50g butter

¾ cup carnaroli rice

2 medium cloves garlic, minced

150ml white wine

75g Parmigiano-Reggiano,
grated

Using good kitchen scissors or poultry shears, remove and discard the chicken wing tips, from the last joint, and the parson's nose. Cut the chicken in half lengthwise, then separate the leg from the breasts on each half. Then cut each breast in half and each thigh piece in half. You should be left with 8 even-sized pieces.

Place the onion, bacon, garlic, thyme and bay leaves in a flame-proof casserole dish, and place the chicken pieces on top. Pour the chardonnay over and marinate overnight in the refrigerator (this is important to give the chicken time to absorb the flavours).

The next day, preheat the oven to 180°C. Add the stock and brandy to the casserole, season with the salt and pepper and bring to the boil over medium heat on the stovetop, then cover and transfer to the oven for 30 minutes.

Remove the lid, add the button mushrooms, cover and cook for a further 30 minutes. Remove from the oven, place the chicken pieces on a serving platter and keep warm.

Strain the liquid into a measuring jug, discarding the thyme and bay leaves. If necessary, top up to 500ml with chicken or vegetable stock. Pour the liquid into a saucepan, then add the strained bacon, mushrooms and onions and set aside for the risotto.

To make the risotto, in a saucepan heat the olive oil and butter until hot, then add the rice and garlic and toast for 3 minutes, stirring continuously with a wooden spoon. Add the wine and let it bubble until absorbed. Stir in ½ cup or 1 ladle of hot reserved chicken liquid, stirring continuously so the rice does not catch. When it is absorbed, continue adding the chicken liquid a ladle at a time and stirring until the liquid has been absorbed before adding more, until the rice is al dente (25–30 minutes). Fold in the bacon, onion and mushrooms from the cooking liquor, add the Parmigiano-Reggiano and adjust the seasoning.

To serve, divide the risotto between the plates and top with the chicken pieces (garnish with parsley or a snow pea shoot if desired).

MEATLOAF

For years now, my friend Bruce has been cooking his mum's meatloaf recipe, which I believe is 'the business'. Meatloaf recipes vary from household to household. Some cooks make it with ground beef, chopped onions, breadcrumbs, an egg to bind it and various spices. Others prefer a mix of ground beef, ground veal and ground pork in equal proportions. Some top the loaf with tomato sauce, others with bacon. Brian's mum's recipe calls for a coffee-flavoured sauce – delicious!

Serves 4

650g minced beef or lamb (or a combination)

500g sausage meat

1 large onion, finely chopped

6 medium cloves garlic, minced

½ green capsicum, cored and roughly chopped

1 tbsp tomato paste

2 small green chillies (optional), finely chopped

6 button mushrooms, sliced

2 tbsp curry powder

1 tbsp each chopped oregano and thyme leaves

½ cup breadcrumbs

2 eggs

1 tbsp olive oil

Sauce

½ cup each Wattie's tomato sauce, malt vinegar and brown sugar

¼ cup each Worcestershire sauce and water

2 tbsp instant coffee powder

Preheat the oven to 180°C. Mix all the loaf ingredients except the olive oil in a large bowl with your hands, combining thoroughly. Form the mixture into a loaf.

Drizzle the oil into a casserole dish, place the loaf in and bake for 1½ hours. After the loaf has cooked for 40 minutes, combine the sauce ingredients in a saucepan and heat to dissolve the sugar (or do this in a suitable container in the microwave). Pour the sauce over the meatloaf and continue cooking, brushing the sauce over the top of the meatloaf every 15 minutes for the remainder of the cooking time.

Remove from the oven and carefully transfer the loaf to a board. Slice and serve with the sauce.

Simon says

If you're keeping an eye on your fat intake, use a disposable aluminium loaf pan. Punch holes in the bottom of the loaf pan before you fill it with the meatloaf mixture. Place the pan on a rack inside a larger baking pan. Excess fat from the meat will drip through the holes into the larger pan.

ASIAN-STYLE FISH FILLETS

I make this dish using baby cucumbers from my local farmers' market in Clevedon. Ginger, garlic, coriander and soy sauce are classic Asian flavours. I use olive oil, which isn't typical; you could use grapeseed oil. This is a great dinner for those nights when you crave something a bit lighter.

Serves 4

2cm fresh ginger, peeled and finely chopped

2 medium cloves garlic, chopped

1 bunch fresh coriander (roots and all), chopped

½ tsp dried chilli flakes (or 1 small red chilli, diced)

¾ cup hot water

½ cup sugar syrup (see recipe below)

2 tbsp sake

½ cup soy sauce

2 tbsp oyster sauce

2 tsp Worcestershire sauce

2 baby cucumbers

800g skinned and boned fresh fish fillets, cut into 200g portions

4 tsp extra virgin olive oil

1 spring onion, finely sliced

4 sprigs coriander to garnish

Sugar Syrup

1 cup sugar

1 cup water

Pound the ginger, garlic, coriander and chilli to a paste using a mortar and pestle, or place all the ingredients in a food processor and blend to a smooth paste. Add the water, sugar syrup, sake, and the soy, oyster and Worcestershire sauces. (This sauce keeps for weeks in the refrigerator, so you can make it in advance and keep on hand.)

Slice the cucumbers into thin rounds and marinate in the sauce for 15 minutes before serving, then strain, reserving the sauce, and set aside.

Preheat the oven to 200°C. Place the fish fillets skin side down on a lightly greased oven tray (line with aluminium foil to reduce the clean-up). Drizzle each piece with 1 teaspoon of olive oil and season with salt and cracked pepper. Place in the oven for 12 minutes or until cooked through. While the fish is cooking, bring the sauce to the boil, adding the spring onion at the last minute.

Place a piece of fish on each plate. Spoon a generous amount of sauce over the fish and top with the reserved cucumber and finish with sprigs of coriander to garnish. Serve with Jasmine Rice (see page 130).

SUGAR SYRUP

In a medium saucepan combine the sugar and water. Bring to the boil, stirring, until the sugar has dissolved. Allow to cool. (This makes more than you need for this recipe, but you can use the remainder in a cocktail.)

Simon says

As an alternative to cooking the fish in the oven, the fish can be pan-fried. Heat a little olive oil in a pan until shimmering (see note page 74). then drop in half a tablespoon of butter. Flour the fish and place each fillet skin-side down on the butter before it melts, and cook both sides to golden brown. Repeat with the remaining fillets.

HAPUKU WITH PARSLEY SAUCE

The sensational sauce that stars in this dish comes from Catalonia in Spain. It's made with egg yolks, bacon, parsley and leeks, and the leeks are reserved and served alongside the fish. Roasting tomatoes concentrates their sugars and enhances their flavour. Their juices are released when they're cut into on the plate, and become part of the sauce.

Serves 4

150ml olive oil

100g rindless streaky bacon, diced

2 large onions, finely diced

8 baby leeks (or the white part of 2 regular leeks cut into 4 x 6cm pieces)

500ml vegetable or fish stock

1 tsp Spanish smoked paprika

½ cup chopped parsley

2 hard-boiled egg yolks, mashed

4 vine-ripened tomatoes

6 baby potatoes, halved

4 x 200g skinned and boned hapuku fillets

4 tbsp butter

Preheat the oven to 180°C.

For the sauce, put 90ml of the oil, the bacon, onions, leeks, stock and paprika in a saucepan and simmer for 30–40 minutes until the onions are perfectly soft and the stock has been reduced by three-quarters. Remove the leeks and set aside in a warm place. Stir the parsley and egg yolks into the bacon and onion mixture, and season with salt. Set aside and keep warm.

Prick the tomatoes 3 times, just around the calyx (stalk and surrounding leaves). Place in an oiled oven tray, place in the oven and roast until the skin begins to blister (8–12 minutes).

Cook the potatoes in salted boiling water until tender. Set aside and keep warm with the leeks.

While the potatoes are cooking, heat 1 tablespoon of the olive oil in a frying-pan until shimmering (see note page 74). Season each piece of hapuku with salt and pepper, drop a tablespoon of butter into the oil then place a fillet of hapuku on top of the butter skin-side up and sauté for 30 seconds on each side. Transfer to an oiled oven tray and repeat the process with the remaining oil, butter and fillets. Bake in the oven for 8–15 minutes, depending on the thickness of the fish fillets.

Arrange 3 halves of potato on each plate with a portion of the leek, a hapuku fillet and a tomato, then sprinkle flaky salt on the tomato. Spoon the sauce over the fish and serve.

MENU

French-inspired dinner

This makes a pretty substantial meal, so tell your guests to arrive hungry. The soup and Cream Caramels can be prepared ahead of time, which is always a help when entertaining.

STARTER

Roast Garlic Soup
(page 22)

MAIN

Coq au Vin on Risotto
(page 127)

DESSERT

Orange Honey Cream Caramels
(page 195)

FILLETS OF FLOUNDER WITH PRAWN MOUSSE AND CHAMPAGNE LEMON SAUCE

I love flounder, but I much prefer eating it in fillets rather than whole because of all the small bones you have to navigate your way around. Either fillet the flounder yourself or find a friendly fishmonger to do it for you. The prawn mousse is also great cooked in a ramekin in a bain-marie and served as an entrée.

Serves 4

270g flounder fillets, skinned and chopped, plus 4 x 170g skinned and boned fillets of flounder

1 egg white

1 tsp salt

pinch of nutmeg

240ml cream

250g chopped prawn meat

2 tbsp chopped curly parsley

4 tsp butter

4 lemon wedges

Champagne Lemon Sauce

125ml sparkling wine (méthode champenoise)

200ml cream

1 tbsp chopped parsley

juice of ½ lemon

Preheat the oven to 185°C.

To make the mousse, in a food processor mince the 270 grams of chopped flounder with the egg white, salt and nutmeg until thoroughly combined. Fold in the cream, prawn meat and parsley.

On an oiled tray, place the flounder fillets skin-side down, and top with the prawn-meat mixture, then place 1 teaspoon of butter on top of each. Place in the oven for 12–15 minutes until the fillets are just opaque and a thin, sharp knife inserted in the mousse comes out hot.

Meanwhile, in a saucepan, simmer the wine until reduced by half, add the cream and reduce by a third. Just before serving, add the parsley and lemon juice.

Remove the fish from the oven and serve on plates. Pour sauce over part of each fillet and place wedges of lemon alongside.

ROAST CHICKEN WITH HERB CHEESE STUFFING

Everyone loves roast chicken, but a great stuffing elevates it to another realm. My herb and cheese stuffing, a delicious combination of celery, Manchego cheese and sage, packs a punch. I heartily recommend that you use Manchego (see below). If you have any left over, eat it on its own or use it in my Bread Dumplings and Tomatoes (see page 37).

Serves 4

30g finely chopped onion

60g finely chopped celery

70g butter

100g white bread cubes

1 tsp freshly ground black pepper

2 eggs, beaten

½ cup (70g) grated Manchego

½ tsp salt

2 tbsp finely chopped fresh sage (or 1 tsp dried sage)

1 x size 20 (2kg) chicken

Preheat the oven to 220°C. In a small frying-pan sauté the onion and celery in the butter until softened. Combine in a large mixing bowl with the bread, pepper, eggs, Manchego, salt and sage.

Pack the cavity of the chicken with the stuffing. Season the skin with salt and pepper, then tie the legs together with butcher's string. Place in a greased and lidded shallow casserole, cover and roast for about 2 hours. Take the lid off for the last 15 minutes to brown.

Remove from the oven. Allow to rest for 10–15 minutes, then carve on a large platter and serve.

Simon says

Manchego cheese is made from the milk of Manchego sheep and is aged for three months or longer. It has a rich golden colour and melts beautifully when cooked. Try cubes of Manchego cheese with fresh pear or with quince paste. Pack cubes of Manchego loosely into a jar and cover with extra virgin olive oil, adding dried herbs such as wild thyme or a little rosemary or even chilli if you like spicy flavours. Seal and leave for a minimum of 1 month before eating. The cheese will continue to mature for up to a year.

PORK HOCK ON MASH WITH MUSTARD AND GREEN PEA SAUCE

This is an old-school dinner that would sell incredibly well in one of my restaurants in the middle of winter. It's a big, hearty dish that is cooked slowly until the meat is falling off the bone. The béchamel-based sauce is a good one to have in your repertoire. Mix the sauce with pasta and it would also taste delicious.

Serves 4

4 cured pork hocks

2 carrots, peeled and chopped

2 stalks celery, roughly chopped

2 bay leaves

6 black peppercorns

2 litres hot water

¼ cup fresh thyme

¼ cup fresh parsley

Green Pea Sauce

5 cups milk

pinch of nutmeg

120g butter

⅔ cup flour

4 tbsp mustard
(use your favourite)

2 cups cooked green peas

Place the hocks in a very large saucepan, cover with water and add the remaining ingredients. Bring to the boil, cover, and simmer for 2 hours or until the meat is about to fall off the bone. Leave the hocks in the cooking liquor and set aside.

To make the sauce, heat the milk and nutmeg in a saucepan until just about to boil, then remove from the heat and set aside. Melt the butter in a saucepan over medium heat, stir in the flour, then gradually add the hot milk, stirring constantly until the mixture thickens. Cook for a further 3 minutes, stirring constantly. Add the mustard and season with salt and freshly ground black pepper. You can adjust the sauce to a thick creamy consistency by adding some of the hock cooking liquor through a sieve. Add the peas just before serving.

Serve the drained hocks on my Mashed Potato (see page 114), then cover with sauce.

SPANISH MEATBALLS

The experience of living in Italy for a year and spending time in Spain has had a big influence on my cooking. This dish, paired with my Saffron Rice (page 178), is the Spanish equivalent of bangers and mash – real comfort food. In Spain the proportion of breadcrumbs to meat varies according to your budget.

Serves 6

450g minced lamb or beef

225g minced pork

1 egg, lightly beaten

4 heaped tbsp breadcrumbs

2 medium cloves garlic, minced

1 medium onion, grated

1 tbsp chopped curly parsley

1 tsp ground cumin

1 tsp ground coriander

pinch of nutmeg

1 cup olive oil

3 tbsp flour

Sauce

60ml olive oil

1 large onion,
halved and thinly sliced

1 red capsicum,
cored and finely chopped

2 medium cloves garlic, minced

2 x 400g cans peeled
tomatoes, crushed

4 tsp dry sherry

3 cinnamon sticks

In a bowl combine the meat, egg, breadcrumbs, garlic, onion, parsley, cumin, coriander and nutmeg, and season with salt and freshly ground black pepper. Mix together until thoroughly combined.

Heat the oil in a frying-pan. With wet hands, roll a small ball of the mixture and dust in flour. Fry until brown all over and cooked through. Remove from the heat and taste to determine whether you have the seasoning correct, adding more salt or pepper if needed. Roll all the mixture into bite-sized balls, dust in flour and fry in the hot oil until browned all over. Set aside.

For the sauce, in a saucepan heat the olive oil and fry the onion, capsicum and garlic over medium heat without browning until the onion is transparent and soft. Add the tomatoes, sherry and cinnamon sticks, bring to a simmer and cook for 20 minutes. Season with salt and black pepper.

Add the meatballs to the sauce and cook gently on low heat for a further 20 minutes. Serve with Saffron Rice (see page 178).

Simon says

Ask your butcher to put the meat through the mincer twice.
If you like a little heat, add some chilli to the meatball mix.

AKAROA SALMON WITH BREAD AND BUTTER POTATO PUDDING

Pan-roasted salmon is served here with a bread and potato pudding nestled under red capsicum. Accompany these with asparagus cooked in water to which you've added a little sugar – guests are sure to comment on how sweet it tastes.

Serves 6

3 red capsicums,
halved and cored

12 slices thin white bread,
generously buttered
on both sides

600g Agria potatoes, peeled

1 tbsp finely chopped onion

2 tbsp butter

3 tbsp cream

6 x 170g pieces salmon, skin on
and pin-boned (see glossary)

2 litres water

6 tbsp sugar

2 tbsp salt

24 spears asparagus

Preheat the oven to 185°C and butter 6 dariole moulds.

Roast the capsicums in the oven skin-side up until thoroughly cooked (about 12 minutes). Place in a plastic bag, seal and leave for 20 minutes. Remove the capsicums from the bag, peel and cut each into 6 pieces large enough to cover the base of the dariole moulds with a little overlap, then place in the bottom of the moulds. Line the moulds with buttered bread and trim level with the lips of the moulds. Set aside.

Boil the potatoes in salted water until cooked well. Drain and mash the potato, and add the onion. Mix in the butter and cream and season with salt and freshly ground black pepper to taste. Fill the moulds to the top with the mash. Set the moulds in a roasting pan of hot water to come halfway up the sides of the moulds, place in the oven and bake for 15 minutes.

Place the salmon skin-side down on a well-oiled oven tray, season with salt and black pepper, then place in the oven, still at 185°C, for 6–9 minutes until cooked to your liking.

In a medium saucepan, bring the water, sugar and salt to the boil, place the asparagus in the pan and cook for 3–5 minutes, depending on how crisp you like your asparagus.

Turn the puddings out onto serving plates, place the asparagus alongside, then the salmon skin-side down, and serve.

MACARONI SAVOURY

Macaroni cheese is something every Kiwi kid grows up loving. I always looked forward to Mum's – although her version didn't include truffle oil. All the other ingredients in this dish are humble, so I reckon you can afford to indulge in a dribble of truffle oil. I also like to use Manchego for a more decadent flavour, or you can use blue cheese or Parmigiano-Reggiano if you like. The breadcrumbs on top are a must.

Serves 2

1 cup macaroni

1 small onion, grated

4 medium tomatoes, sliced

¾ cup grated cheese

2 eggs

1½ cups milk

pinch of nutmeg

⅓ cup fresh breadcrumbs

1 tbsp butter

1 tsp truffle oil

Preheat the oven to 185°C. Boil the macaroni to al dente or according to the packet instructions, then drain thoroughly. Add the onion and season with salt and pepper.

Turn half the mixture into a well-greased casserole, and cover with half the tomato slices and the cheese. Top with the remaining macaroni.

Beat the eggs, milk and nutmeg together and season with salt and pepper. Pour the mixture over the macaroni and top with the remaining tomato. Cover with breadcrumbs, dot with butter and bake for 40 minutes until the top is golden and crisp.

Remove from the oven, drizzle with truffle oil and serve.

Simon says
Cook pasta until it is al dente – an Italian phrase meaning 'to the tooth'. The pasta should offer only a light resistance when bitten into. If it is too soft, it is overcooked.

WHISKY AND MARMALADE CHICKEN

This is such an easy dish to make, and one of those reliable mid-week meals when you want something that tastes great but demands no real effort. The key is to use boneless chicken thighs, as breast meat will end up dry. Serve with buttered leeks and brown rice.

Serves 4

4 tbsp chunky marmalade

1 tbsp water

4 tbsp whisky

4 large boneless chicken thighs

50g butter

200g leeks (white part only), halved lengthwise, well washed and thinly sliced

6 toasted walnuts, roughly chopped

Preheat the oven to 180°C. Combine the marmalade, water and whisky in a bowl, add the chicken, toss to coat, then season with salt and freshly ground black pepper. Place in an ovenproof dish and bake for 30 minutes or until golden.

Melt the butter in a sauté pan and add the leeks. Cook until tender, then season with salt and cracked black pepper.

Serve the chicken alongside boiled brown rice and the buttered leeks. Top with toasted walnuts and drizzle with the pan juices.

Simon says

To clean leeks, soak them in cool salted water. The salt will help to break down the dirt particles and kill any bacteria that remain between the leaves.

sides

DAD'S SILVERBEET

Here's a winning way with a much maligned vegetable (and another, cabbage, gets the same treatment below). Dad is the expert at cooking this, and the small amount of water he uses is the key. You can murder silverbeet and cabbage so easily by overcooking them. Save the stalks from the silverbeet to make Faux Whitebait Fritters (see page 54). The number of servings depends on the number and size of the silverbeet leaves used.

freshly cut and washed
silverbeet leaves

knob of butter

1 tbsp water (optional)

Wash the leaves and cut off the stalk and the thickest portion of rib from each.

Pile the leaves on top of each other and tightly roll up together as you would a newspaper. Hold the leaves in a tight roll and slice as finely as possible into thin ribbons.

Put the butter in a saucepan and pile the silverbeet on top (there should be sufficient water on the leaves from washing, but add a little more if needed). Season with salt and freshly ground black pepper.

Just before serving put the pan on high heat and move the silverbeet around with a fork as it wilts down. Steam for 2–3 minutes, then remove from the heat and cover with a lid. Set aside while you attend to other serving needs. The silverbeet should be just tender. Taste and, if not quite soft enough, give it another burst of steam over the hob.

DAD'S CABBAGE

Cabbage is cabbage and, until you encounter the Savoy variety, not a brassica to get too excited about. Try preparing Savoy cabbage this way to gain a whole new respect for this healthy vegetable. As well as being a superior cabbage, Savoy also retains its colour when cooked.

1 head Savoy cabbage

knob of butter

1 tbsp water (optional)

Wash and cut the thickest portion of rib from the number of leaves required.

Proceed as for silverbeet above, retaining a slight crunchiness for the cabbage to be at its best.

Simon says

Don't be tempted to buy a half cabbage. A half cabbage will have begun to dry out and lose flavour, plus the leaves are in most cases incomplete and more difficult to group and ribbon properly.

MUM'S DUTCH BABIES

Everybody loves Yorkshire puddings; this is our family version of that classic English dish. You can make them whatever size you like – they'll even adapt to being cooked in one large dish. A word of warning, though: avoid putting them too high in the oven, or when they rise they will stick to the top of the oven. Cooked individually, they can be hollowed out and filled with soup. Make the batter at least 4 hours before baking, or a day ahead.

Serves 6

12 large eggs

2 cups flour

1 tsp salt

2 cups milk

60g butter, melted

3 tbsp solid vegetable shortening

Place the eggs, flour, salt, milk and melted butter in a blender, cover and blend for 30 seconds at medium speed until smooth. Scrape the sides with a rubber spatula and blend again.

Cover the batter and set aside for up to 4 hours at room temperature, or chill overnight.

Preheat the oven to 220°C. Using ½ tablespoon of shortening for each, grease 6 x 400ml ovenproof ramekins and place in the oven for 5 minutes or until super-hot.

Pour the batter into the ramekins and bake for 15 minutes. Reduce the oven temperature to 180°C and bake a further 5–10 minutes until the edges are puffed and golden.

Remove from the oven and serve immediately.

Simon says

To test whether eggs are fresh, place them in a bowl of cold water. A really fresh egg will sink to the bottom and lay on its side. Older eggs will stand upright in the water and really old eggs may even float.

BACON AND KUMARA PIE

This pie takes kumara to the next level. Serve it as an accompaniment to lamb chops, eye fillet or chicken, or at any barbecue. It's also a great dish to serve as an entrée.

Serves 2

3 large kumara

2 rashers rindless bacon

3 tbsp finely chopped onion

1 tbsp butter

2 apples, peeled and grated

½ cup grated cheese

2 tbsp pine nuts

Preheat the oven to 180°C and bake the kumara whole with the skins on until well cooked. Once cooked, cool, remove the skins and place the kumara in a bowl.

Sauté the bacon in a pan until crisp. Set aside.

Sauté the onion in the butter until translucent, then add to the kumara along with the apple and half the bacon. Mix well and season with salt and freshly ground black pepper.

Place the mixture in an ovenproof dish (or 2 individual ramekins) and cover with cheese. Toast the pine nuts in a dry frying-pan until golden. Scatter the reserved bacon and the pine nuts on top of the cheese and place in the oven (still at 180°C) for 15 minutes. Remove from the oven and serve.

CREAMED CORN

Creamed Corn is a bit of a Kiwi classic. The key to making it creamy is to use homogenised milk. This makes a fantastic side dish for summer barbecues. It's also a great breakfast served on toasted ciabatta.

Serves 8

600g frozen corn kernels

230ml cream

230ml homogenised milk

1 tsp salt

3 tbsp sugar

pinch of cayenne or white pepper

2 tbsp melted butter

2 tbsp flour

8 slices ciabatta, chargrilled

freshly grated Parmigiano-Reggiano to serve

Combine the corn, cream, milk, salt, sugar and cayenne in a saucepan, bring to the boil and simmer for 5 minutes.

Blend the butter and flour, add to the corn and mix in well, then cook for a further 5 minutes, stirring constantly. Remove from the heat.

Place a piece of warm chargrilled ciabatta on each of 8 plates, spoon a generous amount of Creamed Corn on top and sprinkle with Parmigiano-Reggiano.

Simon says

As a variation, place the Creamed Corn in a casserole, sprinkle with Parmigiano-Reggiano and place under a grill until evenly browned.

MENU
weeknight dinner for friends

This is the perfect menu for when you're entertaining mid-week and you need a meal that comes together quickly. You can pass the Chipotle Mussels around to guests while you're preparing the chicken and vegetables. The Mango Whisky Parfait could be made in the morning and kept in the refrigerator until you're ready to serve it.

STARTER

Chipotle Mussels
(page 27)

MAIN

Dad's Sage Chicken
(page 95)

SIDES

Dad's Cabbage
(page 156)

Creamed Corn
(page 163)

DESSERT

Mango and Whisky Parfait
(page 198)

CREAMED SPINACH

This dish has been on the menu at my Auckland steak restaurant, Jervois Steak House, since it opened. It's a rich dish made with lots of cream, but is a winning accompaniment to steak or served on toast. Make sure you squeeze all the excess water out of the spinach and chop it finely.

Serves 6

1 tbsp butter

1 large onion, finely diced

1½ litres cream

500g spinach, blanched, squeezed dry and finely chopped

1 cup milk

½ tsp nutmeg

Melt the butter in a heavy-based saucepan, add the onion and sauté until soft and translucent (about 4 minutes). Add the cream and bring to the boil. Reduce the heat to low and simmer until the cream is reduced by half.

Add the spinach and blend roughly with a stick blender, thinning the mixture with milk until the desired consistency is achieved (mine is the consistency of thick custard). Season to taste with nutmeg, flaky salt and freshly ground white pepper. Serve in a bowl.

BELL HOUSE POTATOES

When I did my apprenticeship at Tony Astle's restaurant, Antoine's, in Auckland I made this rich, creamy potato dish every day. So when I opened my first restaurant, Bell House in Howick, I simply had to put it on the menu.

Serves 6–8

60g butter

2.1kg potatoes, peeled and thinly sliced into rounds

2 cups grated cheese

2 medium onions, finely sliced

1 cup milk

1 cup cream

pinch of nutmeg

¼ tsp paprika

Preheat the oven to 190°C. Grease a deep baking dish or casserole with half the butter. Layer the potatoes, cheese and onions in the dish, seasoning each layer and ending with potato (reserve enough cheese to sprinkle over the top).

Combine the milk, cream and nutmeg in a saucepan and heat to boiling point, then pour onto the potatoes to come about two-thirds of the way up the side of the dish. Dot the top with the remaining butter and sprinkle with paprika and the grated cheese.

Bake on the top shelf of the oven for about 1 hour or until the potatoes are tender and the top is golden brown.

Simon says

Store cheese in a sealed container with two lumps of sugar to prevent it going mouldy.

KUMARA-STUFFED TOMATOES

I doubt this kumara stuffing is something you would expect to find in your average tomato, but it's a wicked combination of flavours. Be sure to use good-quality, vine-ripened tomatoes. Look for them at your local farmers' market. This is a great side dish to serve with Oyster-stuffed Chicken (see page 82).

Serves 4

300g peeled and finely diced orange Beauregard kumara

extra virgin olive oil for drizzling

1 tbsp capers, chopped (if packed in salt, rinse well)

2 courgettes, peeled and grated

½ cup grated Parmigiano-Reggiano

4 large tomatoes, halved, cored and seeded

curly parsley leaves to garnish

Preheat the oven to 180°C. Place the kumara in a casserole dish, drizzle with olive oil and bake in the oven until tender (15–20 minutes).

In a bowl combine the kumara with the capers, courgettes and Parmigiano-Reggiano. Stuff the tomato halves with the mixture, season with salt and pepper and drizzle with olive oil. Bake for about 10 minutes and serve topped with curly parsley leaves.

Simon says

Kumara should be stored in a cool, dark place. Do not refrigerate as they will suffer 'chilling injury', which presents as shrivelling, increased decay, surface pitting and sometimes a hard core which fails to soften on cooking.

ORANGE AND RED ONION SALAD

You will find this salad served in Spain in winter months when other ingredients are in short supply. Personally, I love it in summer or winter.

Serves 6

6 large oranges

1 tbsp cumin seeds

½ tsp freshly ground black pepper

1 tsp chopped fresh mint, plus 2 sprigs for garnish

120ml extra virgin olive oil

90ml orange juice

1 small red onion, thinly sliced into rings

12 olives (use your favourites)

Using a sharp knife, remove the peel and pith from the oranges then slice into thin rounds.

In a bowl mix together the cumin seeds, black pepper, mint, olive oil and orange juice. Season with a sprinkling of flaky salt to taste. Set aside.

In a serving dish arrange the oranges and onion, drizzle the dressing over and scatter with olives and sprigs of mint. Allow to rest for 2 hours before serving.

Simon says
It is important to let the salad rest, which allows the onion to soften slightly, and all the flavours to develop.

MINTED COUSCOUS SALAD

It's always good to have a few interesting salads up your sleeve to serve at a barbecue. Quick to rustle up and full of flavour, this is one of my favourites.

Serves 6

2 cups water

250g couscous

1 cucumber, peeled, seeded and chopped

220g goat's feta, crumbled

5 tomatoes, roughly chopped

½ cup finely chopped parsley

½ cup black olives

¼ cup finely chopped fresh mint

In a saucepan, bring the water to the boil then add the couscous. Remove from the heat, cover and allow to stand for 6 minutes. Transfer to a bowl, allow to cool then add the remaining ingredients and season with salt and freshly ground black pepper to taste.

SAFFRON RICE

This flavoured rice, cooked in stock rather than water, goes brilliantly with my Spanish Meatballs (see page 145). It would also be great with any meat dish with bold flavours.

Serves 6–8

2 cups basmati rice

3 pinches of saffron threads

¼ cup white wine

2 tbsp olive oil

1 small onion, finely chopped

3½ cups chicken or vegetable stock

1 tsp salt

Rinse the rice in a colander, drain and set aside. Place the saffron and white wine in a small saucepan, bring to the boil then remove from the heat and set aside.

In a medium saucepan heat the olive oil, add the onion and sauté until soft, then add the rice, sauté for 1 minute, stirring, then add the saffron and wine, stock and salt. Stir to combine, then cover and cook for 20 minutes until the rice is tender. Fluff up the rice with a fork just before serving.

JASMINE RICE

Lots of people have theories on how to cook perfect rice. This is my tried and trusted method if you don't have a rice cooker. The ratio of water to rice is the crucial factor.

Serves 6–8

4 cups water

2 cups jasmine rice, washed

1 tbsp butter

pinch of salt

Bring the water to the boil in a medium saucepan and slowly stir in the rice, butter and salt. Cover the saucepan, lower the heat and gently simmer for 20–25 minutes, depending on the desired softness of the rice.

TAMARILLO CHUTNEY

Homemade chutney is great to have on hand to serve with anything from cheese to ham or chicken. And if you're going to make chutney, you can't beat this tamarillo version – it goes with everything and adds extra magic to burgers in particular. It's also great to have some spare jars of chutney to give away.

Makes 1.2kg

12 tamarillos

350g apples, chopped

350g onions, chopped

1 cup malt vinegar

1 heaped tsp mixed spice

1 tbsp flaky salt

2¼ cups brown sugar

1 tsp cayenne

Steep the tamarillos in boiling water for 5 minutes, then peel with a small, sharp knife and chop. Combine in a saucepan with the remaining ingredients and boil over moderate heat for about 2 hours, stirring occasionally to prevent the mixture sticking, until the chutney has a jam-like consistency. Remove from the heat, cool, then bottle in sterilised jars.

Simon says

To sterilise jars, place the jars in a large saucepan and cover with water. Bring to the boil and boil for 10 minutes. Remove from the heat and leave jars to stand in the water until they are ready to fill.

PICKLED HONEY MUSHROOMS

These are excellent as part of an antipasto platter to snack on while you're standing around the barbecue waiting for someone to overcook the sausages. Serve in a small dish and garnish with fresh thyme.

Serves 6

2 tbsp olive oil

500g whole button mushrooms

12 whole garlic gloves, peeled

3 tbsp manuka honey

100ml red wine vinegar

fresh thyme sprigs

¼ tsp flaky salt

Heat the oil in a shallow frying-pan and cook the mushrooms until coloured, then add the garlic and cook for a further 3 minutes. Add the honey and allow to simmer for a few minutes until the mushrooms begin to caramelise. Add the vinegar and thyme, and season with salt and cracked black pepper. Cool before placing in an airtight container. Store in the refrigerator for up to 3 weeks.

Simon says

To store fresh mushrooms keep them in a brown paper bag in the refrigerator, but they are best used as soon as possible.

desserts

APPLE FRITTERS WITH CARAMEL SAUCE

Without doubt, this is a sinful dessert. If you're feeling completely wicked, try adding 50ml of rum to the sauce. And naturally, Caramel Sauce calls for ice-cream to be served on the side.

Serves 4

1 cup flour

1 tsp custard powder

¼ tsp salt

2 tsp sugar

1 egg

50ml milk

1 tsp baking powder

3 apples, peeled and grated

large knob of butter

1 lemon

Caramel Sauce

½ cup sugar

1 tbsp water

½ cup cream

To make the sauce, place the sugar and water in a heavy-based saucepan and heat, without stirring, until the sugar has turned a golden caramel colour, swirling the pan occasionally so the mixture colours evenly. Using a wooden spoon, slowly stir in the cream, then bring to the boil again to ensure no lumps remain (the sugar gets very hot, so be careful). Set aside. (This can be made a day in advance.)

Place the flour, custard powder, salt and sugar in a basin. Mix in the egg and milk, then the baking powder.

Mix the apples into the batter and combine well. Melt the butter in a large frying-pan over moderate heat, then drop tablespoonfuls of batter into the pan and fry until golden brown on both sides.

Pile the fritters onto a plate, then pour the Caramel Sauce over and grate lemon zest over the top. Serve with ice-cream if desired.

STRAWBERRIES IN SNOW

When local strawberries hit the shelves, give this dessert a whirl. They are the star here, so don't be tempted to use the pale imported strawberries. The addition of rosewater really makes this dessert.

Serves 4

250g fresh strawberries, hulled and halved

2 tbsp brandy

2 egg whites

½ cup sugar

300ml cream

4 drops rosewater

Marinate the strawberries in the brandy for 30 minutes.

Whisk the egg whites, adding the sugar slowly until stiff peaks form.

Whip the cream until stiff, then mix in the brandy from the strawberries along with the rosewater. Combine the strained strawberries with the whipped cream mixture, then fold in the egg whites, place in the fridge for 4 hours and serve in sundae glasses or small bowls.

Simon says
You'll find bottles of imported rosewater in specialty food stores.

SIMON GAULT'S MOLTEN CHOCOLATE PUDDINGS

These have been on the menu at my restaurant Euro for ever. Believe it or not, they are best cooked in an old baked bean can. Remove both ends from the can so you end up with a metal cylinder. Put the wider end (without the lip) on the oven tray and they will turn out perfectly. The secret is to have a molten centre so it oozes out over the plate when cut into. You can make the mixture and store it in the fridge in a disposable piping bag for around a month, so when guests arrive you can cook the puddings and look like a star.

Serves 6

5 eggs

5 yolks

⅓ cup sugar

250g dark chocolate (at least 72% cocoa solids)

250g butter, plus extra for the moulds

3 tbsp flour

2 tbsp cocoa powder

icing sugar for dusting

Using an electric beater, whisk the eggs and yolks with the sugar until thick and pale.

Melt the chocolate and butter in a double-boiler or in a stainless steel bowl over a saucepan of boiling water, stirring constantly to prevent burning. Fold the melted chocolate mixture into the egg mixture until combined and of an even consistency.

Sift the flour over the mix and fold in until completely incorporated with no lumps. Transfer the mixture to a piping bag and place in the refrigerator until firm.

Butter 6 baked bean cans (or dariole moulds), lightly dust with cocoa powder and place on a tray or baking paper. Once the mixture is firm, pipe into the moulds, then refrigerate until set.

Preheat the oven to 185°C. Place the chocolate puddings on an oven tray and bake for 16 minutes. Remove from the oven and, very importantly, allow them to stand for 3 minutes before turning them out, to avoid cracking. Turn out the puddings onto individual plates and dust with icing sugar.

Simon says
Use empty 210g baked bean cans with the top and bottom removed instead of special dariole moulds.

GOLDEN SYRUP PUDDING

I have fond memories of eating this pudding at my grandmother's house. As a kid I was always enthralled by how the golden syrup soaks down through the pudding to form a topping when the pudding is turned out on a plate. It's delicious served warm with ice-cream or cold the next day for afternoon tea – if you're lucky enough to have any left over.

Serves 6

85g butter, softened

½ tsp grated lemon zest

⅓ cup sugar

2 eggs

⅓ cup flour

¼ tsp baking powder

¼ tsp flaky salt

¼ cup milk

4 tbsp golden syrup

Beat together the butter, lemon zest and sugar until light and fluffy. Add the eggs one at a time, beating well after each addition. Fold in the flour, baking powder and salt, then add just enough milk to give a soft dropping consistency. Pour the golden syrup into the bottom of a well-buttered or non-stick pudding basin, then pour in the batter. Cover with the basin lid, or well-buttered aluminium foil or a pudding cloth, tying securely in place.

Quarter fill with water a saucepan large enough to hold the pudding basin and bring to the boil. Lower in the pudding basin, cover and steam for 1½ hours. Check from time to time and top up the saucepan with more boiling water if necessary.

Serve warm with Easy Honey Ice-cream (see page 218).

ORANGE HONEY CREAM CARAMELS

This is a tangy variation of the classic French crème caramel. It's always better made a day or two in advance so that when you turn it out, the cream dessert doesn't stick to the bottom of the ramekin and the caramel oozes out. Honey and cardamom are a perfect marriage of flavours.

Serves 4

260g honey

1 tbsp water

4 eggs

550ml milk

finely grated zest of ½ orange

½ tsp ground cardamom

Preheat the oven to 160°C. Heat two-thirds of the honey with the water in a small, heavy-based saucepan, stirring as the honey comes to the boil. Reduce the heat to medium and watch carefully until it turns rich and golden. As soon as the colour deepens, remove from the heat and allow the bubbles to subside, then divide the mixture between 4 small ramekins.

Warm the remaining honey, whisk in the eggs until just combined, then whisk in the milk, orange zest and cardamom. Pour the mixture evenly over the honey caramel in the ramekins. Place the ramekins in a bain-marie or roasting dish filled with water coming halfway up the outside of the ramekins, and cover the dish with aluminium foil. Bake for 20–30 minutes until the custards are just set. Remove from the water bath, cool, then refrigerate for 1–2 days. Remove from the refrigerator 1 hour before serving. Invert onto plates to serve.

POTS DE CRÈME AU CHOCOLAT

Not for the faint-hearted, these are so incredibly rich you could probably serve one between three guests. Chocolate fans will think they've died and gone to heaven. At Christmas time, serve them like a sweet pâté with warm panettone.

Serves 6

1 cup semi-sweet chocolate chips (I use 70% cocoa solids)

1½ cups scalded cream (heated until just before boiling)

2 egg yolks

2 tbsp brandy

Rum Sauce (see page 211)

Place all the ingredients except the Rum Sauce in a blender and blitz on high speed until smooth.

Pour the mixture into 6 small ramekins, demitasse cups or espresso cups, top each with a teaspoon of rum sauce and chill for 3 hours before serving. Biscotti make a great accompaniment.

MANGO AND WHISKY PARFAIT

I've based this dessert on *atholl brose*, a traditional Scottish drink made with oatmeal and whisky, I've added mango and changed the name. If you can't get fresh mango, substitute any other fruit. It's a bit of a boozy dessert so probably not one to serve to the kids, but for adults feel free to add more whisky. Make it at least an hour in advance so the oats soften. It can also be made a day ahead.

Serves 6

¾ cup rolled oats

80ml cream

60ml whisky

100g honey

200g fresh mango, chopped, plus extra slices to garnish

Preheat the oven to 180°C. Place the rolled oats in a roasting pan and toast in the oven until just a little coloured, stirring occasionally so they toast evenly. Once toasted, sift the oats to remove the dust.

Whisk the cream to soft peaks, add the whisky, honey, mango and rolled oats to the cream and fold in until well combined. Chill before serving in small bowls or glasses, topped with mango slices.

GINGER PUDDING WITH CUSTARD COINTREAU CREAM

This delicious pudding is based on a recipe of my grandmother's, although I don't recall her adding Cointreau to the cream. It's a super-easy recipe; the only time involved is in the cooking.

Serves 4

110g butter

1 cup flour

1 tsp mixed spice

1 tsp ground ginger

½ cup sultanas

½ cup golden syrup, warmed

½ cup milk with ½ tsp baking soda

Custard Cointreau Cream

55g butter, softened

2 cups icing sugar

2 tbsp custard powder

2 tbsp hot water

2 tbsp Cointreau

zest of ½ orange

Rub the butter into the flour until well incorporated and crumbly. Add the mixed spice, ginger, sultanas and golden syrup, then mix in the milk and dissolved baking soda. Pour the batter into a well-buttered or non-stick pudding basin. Cover with the basin lid, or well-buttered aluminium foil or a pudding cloth, tied securely in place.

Quarter fill with water a saucepan large enough to hold the pudding basin and bring to the boil. Lower in the pudding basin, cover and steam for 2 hours. Check from time to time and top up the saucepan with more boiling water if necessary.

For the custard cream, cream the butter, icing sugar, custard powder and hot water, then mix in the Cointreau and orange zest. Place in a bowl and top with a little more zest.

Serve the pudding warm, with the Custard Cointreau Cream.

PINEAPPLE DELIGHT

The first time Mum made this, she was just married. She mistook the tablespoon of rice for a pound . . . *uh oh*. I'm happy to report that she has made it many times since, with great success. It's one of those slightly old-fashioned desserts that become the stuff of great memories.

Serves 4

1 tbsp short-grain rice

1 cup sugar

pinch of salt

1 tsp vanilla essence or ¼ tsp vanilla extract

425g can pineapple, drained, reserving syrup, and fruit roughly chopped

1 tbsp gelatine

1 cup hot water

300ml cream, stiffly whipped

Fresh As freeze-dried raspberries to serve (optional; available from supermarkets)

In a small saucepan, boil the rice in water until quite soft. Drain and place in a bowl with the sugar, salt and vanilla. Add the pineapple syrup, then the fruit. Dissolve the gelatine in the hot water, add to the mixture, stir and put aside to set.

When the mixture is thoroughly cold and beginning to set, fold the whipped cream in until well blended. Serve in bowls and top with freeze-dried raspberries, if desired.

TREACLE TARTS

It doesn't get much better than these Treacle Tarts served with a dollop of mascarpone. Make sure you don't overmix the pastry, or it won't have the satisfying short texture required.

Serves 6

Pastry

4 cups flour

250g butter

pinch of salt

90ml water

Filling

5 eggs

¾ cup breadcrumbs

425ml (570g) golden syrup

140ml (205g) treacle

280ml cream

zest of 1 lemon

2 green apples, peeled and grated

6 tbsp fresh mascarpone to serve

For the pastry, in a food processor place the flour, butter and salt and blitz until the mixture has a fine crumb consistency. Add the water and briefly blitz again just until incorporated. Remove from the processor and gently press the pastry together into a ball shape, wrap in plastic wrap and rest in the fridge for 30 minutes.

For the filling, in a mixing bowl, place the eggs, breadcrumbs, golden syrup, treacle and cream, then mix well. Mix in the lemon zest and apples and set aside.

Remove the pastry from the fridge and roll out to a thickness of 2–3mm, then use the pastry to line 6 x 10cm tart tins. Wrap with plastic wrap and place in the fridge to rest for 30 minutes.

Preheat the oven to 185°C. Remove the tins from the fridge, line with baking paper and add baking rice or beans. Blind bake the pastry cases in the oven for 15 minutes. Remove from the oven and take out the baking paper and rice. Spoon the treacle mixture into the pastry cases, return to the oven and bake for a further 25 minutes. Remove from the oven and allow to cool. Take the tarts out of the tins, place on serving plates and top each with a tablespoon of mascarpone.

Simon says

To blind bake tart cases, line the uncooked case with baking paper and fill with uncooked rice, dried beans or baking beans. Bake the pastry as required and then remove the paper and filling. This results in a crisp pastry shell.

MENU
seafood lovers' dinner

This would make a romantic celebration dinner, so long as your lover loves seafood! The entrée comes from Venice – one of the most romantic cities in the world – and the Crayfish Thermidor main is the ultimate indulgence to share with someone special. What else could follow but a rich, creamy chocolate dessert.

STARTER

Venetian-style Prawns
(page 65)

MAIN

Crayfish Thermidor
(page 91)

DESSERT

Pots de Crème au Chocolat
(page 196)

HOT CHOCOLATE SAUCE

Golden syrup is the secret ingredient in this scrumptious sauce (opposite); and if you want to sneak in some brandy, be my guest. Serve with vanilla or Easy Honey Ice-cream (see page 218).

Serves 4

20g cocoa

20g butter

½ cup hot water

1 cup sugar

1 tbsp golden syrup

In a saucepan, place the cocoa, butter and water, bring to the boil, then add the sugar and golden syrup and boil for 3 minutes until roughly the consistency of golden syrup.

Serve with ice-cream, with some grated chocolate over the top.

RUM SAUCE

Whenever you want to serve custard, flash it up with this version. It's great with Ellerie's steamed Christmas Pudding (see page 214).

Serves 8

1 cup cream

2 egg yolks

1 tbsp sugar

3 tbsp dark rum

½ cup cream, whipped

In the microwave or in a small saucepan on the stovetop, heat the cream until small bubbles appear. In a separate glass bowl mix the egg yolks and sugar until creamy. Pour the cream over the egg mixture, whisking constantly. Return to the microwave or saucepan and cook, stirring with a wooden spoon, until the mixture coats the back of the spoon. Cool, then add the rum and fold in the whipped cream. Place in a jug and set aside until ready to serve.

FRUIT SALAD DELUXE

A lighter-style dessert to serve at the end of a meal, this is a clever way to transform a fruit salad with a lemon curd-like cream that adds that extra magic. Make it with any of your favourite fruits.

Makes about 2 cups cream

⅔ cup sugar

2 tbsp flour

2 eggs, beaten

2 tbsp grapeseed oil

3 tbsp lemon juice

4 tbsp orange juice

1 cup pineapple juice

½ cup cream, whipped to soft peaks

selection of seasonal fruit, chopped

Combine the sugar and flour in the top of a double-boiler or stainless steel bowl over a saucepan of boiling water, then add the remaining ingredients except the cream and fruit. Stir constantly until thickened. Remove from the heat and set aside to cool. When cold, fold in the whipped cream.

Place the fruit salad in small serving glasses, and pour the deluxe mix over the top or serve in a bowl on the side.

ELLERIE'S CHRISTMAS PUDDING

My mum, Ellerie, makes this pudding for Christmas Day, in the traditional way with a button and foil-wrapped coins buried in the centre. Legend has it that the recipient of the button will remain a bachelor, while those served up coins are going to be lucky for the next year. It's best cooked several weeks in advance and and fed with a couple of tablespoons of rum or brandy every couple of days. Don't forget to pour heated brandy over the pudding just before serving – light it and carry the flaming pudding to the table. Serve it with Rum Sauce (see page 211).

Serves 8

220g breadcrumbs

220g butter, melted

¾ cup sugar

4 tsp golden syrup

2 drops each vanilla and almond essence

1¼ cups flour, sifted

salt

1kg mixed fruit

1 tsp baking soda

1½ cups milk, warmed

brandy for flaming

Rum Sauce (see page 211)

Place the breadcrumbs in a bowl and pour the melted butter over. Mix to combine, then add the sugar, golden syrup and essences. Cool a little before mixing in the flour, salt and mixed fruit. Dissolve the baking soda in the milk, add to the mixture and mix well to combine.

Pour the batter into a well-buttered or non-stick pudding basin. Cover with the basin lid, or well buttered aluminium foil or a pudding cloth, tied securely in place.

Quarter fill with water a saucepan large enough to hold the pudding basin and bring to the boil. Lower in the pudding basin, cover and steam for 2 hours. Check from time to time and top up the saucepan with more boiling water if necessary.

Turn out onto a plate and decorate with fresh holly if available. Pour some brandy over, set it alight and carry it to the table. Serve with Rum Sauce.

EASY HONEY ICE-CREAM

To me, one of the greatest things we have in New Zealand is our unique honey, and this ice-cream is a great way to showcase it, be it manuka, pohutukawa or whatever your favourite is. No ice-cream maker is required for this recipe, although it will always turn out best if you do have one.

Serves 12

1.2 litres milk

1¾ cups sugar

4 tbsp cornflour

½ tsp salt

6 medium eggs

2 cups evaporated milk

100ml honey

1 tsp vanilla essence or ¼ tsp vanilla extract

60ml aged balsamic vinegar (optional)

In a medium saucepan, bring 1 litre of the milk and the sugar to a simmer. Mix the cornflour, 100ml of the milk and the salt to a paste. Add to the scalded milk, stirring until the sugar is dissolved. Simmer over low heat for 20 minutes, stirring constantly, until thickened.

Beat the eggs, then beat in the remaining 100ml milk. Stir the hot milk mixture into the egg mixture. Return to the saucepan and cook over low heat, stirring constantly with a wooden spoon, until the mixture coats the back of the spoon. Cool, then add the evaporated milk, honey and vanilla. Pour into an old ice-cream container and freeze overnight. (Churn the ice-cream at this point if you have an ice-cream maker.)

If the ice-cream gets too hard, cut into small pieces and briefly blitz in a food processor until smooth. Serve in parfait glasses, topped with a tablespoon of aged balsamic vinegar if desired.

GRAPEFRUIT WHIP

When I was a kid I always used to look forward to Mum making this dessert, which separates into two layers – jelly-like on the bottom and like a light soufflé on top. It's really simple, but impressive. Serve it in a big dish or in individual glasses. If you can't get grapefruit, use oranges instead.

Serves 6

1 tbsp gelatine

½ cup hot water

3 eggs, separated

1 cup sugar

1 cup grapefruit juice

grated zest of 1 grapefruit

Dissolve the gelatine in the hot water.

Beat the egg yolks with the sugar until light and creamy. Add the juice and zest and mix well, then add the gelatine mixture and combine thoroughly.

Whisk the egg whites to stiff peaks, then whisk into the grapefruit mixture. Pour into a glass serving dish, place in the fridge and allow to set for 3–4 hours. The mix will separate into two layers. When ready, serve in parfait glasses.

WILD BERRY EGGNOG

More the perfect brunch or Christmas morning drink than a dessert, this is breakfast in a glass with liqueur. What could be nicer?

Serves 6

½ punnet strawberries

1 punnet blackberries

360ml manuka honey liqueur

1 cup ice

1½ tsp vanilla extract

360ml cream

1 tbsp brown sugar

180ml cranberry juice

6 eggs

nutmeg to garnish (optional)

Place the berries and liqueur in a blender with the ice, and process until smooth. Add the vanilla, cream, sugar and cranberry juice, blend to combine, then add the eggs and blend again. Pour into small tumbler glasses and dust with nutmeg if desired.

FIVE PER CENT MAGIC INGREDIENTS

In my cooking I am always looking for that 'five per cent magic' – the taste sensation that transforms a dish into something sublime. I wouldn't be without the ingredients on these pages. I heartily recommend that you give them a try.

Carnaroli rice: Carnaroli is my rice of choice for risotto. It is a medium-grain rice grown in the Vercelli province of northern Italy. Carnaroli differs from the more common Arborio rice due to its higher starch content and firmer texture. It keeps its shape better than other forms of rice during the slow cooking required for making risotto. It is often described as 'superfino' rice or 'the king of rices'.

Buffalo mozzarella: Buffalo milk mozzarella originated in Italy but in New Zealand you can now buy excellent mozzarella from Clevedon Valley Buffalo Company, made with milk from water buffalo herds in south Auckland. This is the only local fresh mozzarella that is made in the traditional Italian way. Buffalo mozzarella from Campania in Italy bears the 'Mozzarella di Bufala Campana' trademark. The Consortium for the Protection of the Buffalo Cheese of Campania is an organisation of about 200 producers, who, under Italian law, are responsible for the 'protection, surveillance, promotion and marketing' of Mozzarella di Bufala Campana. Mozzarella should never be eaten directly out of the fridge because it will have no flavour. Let it rest at room temperature for at least half an hour and you will taste the difference.

Murray River sea salt: Salt is a matter of personal taste and preference. I suggest you try different salts to find one that you like.

My salt of choice is Murray River Gourmet Sea Salt Flakes, harvested from pure underground saline waters in Australia's Murray–Darling river basin. It is a high-quality salt with unique flavour and a delicate pink colour, and I like the way the soft flakes allow easy crumbling over plates for added seasoning.

We use this sea salt in all of our restaurants and it attracts lots of favourable comments for both its flavour and appearance.

Truffle oil: This amazingly pungent oil is infused with flavour from the addition of white or black truffle. It is delicious drizzled over mash, roast potatoes, barbecued meat, risotto, soups – in fact, just about anything savoury – just before serving. It is not an oil to cook with but should be used as a condiment. The aroma and flavour of truffle oil are gloriously intense and unmistakable. I cook with truffle oil from Alba in Italy – one magic ingredient that I wouldn't be without.

Stock: A good stock is the foundation of many great dishes – risotto, casseroles, sauces and soups in particular. When I'm cooking at home I don't always have the time to make fresh stock, which is why I've developed a range of pre-prepared vegetable, beef and chicken stocks under the Simon Gault Home Cuisine range. Made with quality fresh ingredients and a long, slow reduction they are even good enough to drink straight as a soup.

Parmigiano-Reggiano: Recognised as the 'king of cheeses', Parmigiano-Reggiano has been around for some 900 years. It is still made in the same way and true Parmigiano-Reggiano will always bear a stamp of origin and date of production. This way you can work out its age. My company imports Parmigiano-Reggiano from Figli di Bruno Cantarelli, which is guaranteed to have been aged for 24 months. Nothing rivals the intense flavour of authentic Parmigiano-Reggiano, which imbues any dish with added flavour. Try it shaved over a rocket salad, stirred into a risotto, grated over pasta dishes, or served in slivers with slices of pear, either as a pre-dinner snack or instead of dessert.

Honey: Honey is a wonderful sweetener in sweet or savoury foods. I cook with it from breakfast through to dinner time. Just like salt, you need to taste different honeys to find one that you like.

Balsamic vinegar: True balsamic vinegar comes from Modena in Italy. The best balsamic is a rich syrup of molasses-like consistency aged for anything from 12 to more than 50 years. The making of true balsamic has remained unchanged for centuries and it is protected in the same way as that of Parmigiano-Reggiano. The 'must' begins its life maturing in a barrel with an opening covered by a linen napkin so as to allow evaporation. Each year as a result of evaporation the contents are moved to decreasingly smaller barrels until it is ready for bottling. I import and use a balsamic that comes from a fifth-generation company in Modena that has been producing balsamic vinegars for 150 years. There are bottles labelled balsamic vinegar in New Zealand supermarkets, but they are nothing like the luxurious syrup that is true balsamic.

Rubs: Spice rubs are a great and easy way to transform a cut of meat into something really special. When I first opened my restaurant Euro in 2000 I developed a rub for rotisserie chicken, and it has become one of those signature dishes I will never take off the menu. It's a rub that goes with everything – chicken, prawns, veggies, mince, roast potatoes . . . the list is endless. Now that rub and two others are available in supermarkets as part of my Simon Gault Home Cuisine range.

Prosciutto crudo: When buying prosciutto, always look for the coveted crown 'Prosciutto di Parma' either on the packaging or on the ham itself. This guarantees that it hails from Parma in Italy, where it is made from locally raised pigs fed a strict diet including whey from locally made Parmigiano-Reggiano cheese. Using the best pigs that eat the right foods makes a perfect ham. Prosciutto has a delicate salty taste that transforms all manner of dishes. It is wonderful in a toasted sandwich, wrapped around cooked beans or asparagus, or laid over the skin of a chicken before roasting.

CHEF'S NOTES

Basic ingredients

Throughout this book unless otherwise stated:
Flour is standard or plain flour
Sugar is caster sugar
Butter is salted
Eggs are size 7

Seasoning

Season dishes according to your taste. In some recipes you will see that I don't add seasoning at all. As the inclusion of ingredients such as olives and capers contributes sufficient saltiness.

I recommend that you taste every dish before you serve it. Ladle a small amount of the mixture into a dish and taste it. Add a little salt and taste it again. If it tastes better, then add some salt to the main mixture until you achieve the same taste. Keep adding salt to your test dish until it tastes right, and remember that taste is quite personal. You can always add more seasoning, so add salt sparingly each time you season a dish.

If you add too much salt to soup by mistake, add some sliced potatoes and simmer for a further 10–15 minutes. Remove the potatoes before serving; they will have absorbed the salt.

Cooking meat

Meat should be at room temperature before cooking, so remove it from the refrigerator an hour ahead of time, depending on the size of the piece you will be cooking.

A meat thermometer is the most accurate way to test whether meat is properly cooked and it is a good investment in any home kitchen. An internal temperature of 42°C indicates the meat is rare, 58°C equates to medium-rare and 68°C is medium-well done. Pork should be cooked to between 71°C and 74°C.

Always rest meat for 15 minutes after cooking to retain moistness.

Storing vegetables

Don't spoil the flavour of tomatoes by storing them in the refrigerator. Keep ripe tomatoes in a cool place but not below 12°C. Tomatoes that have been picked too early can be stored in a brown paper bag at room temperature. They will ripen in a day or two.

To ripen avocados, place them in a bag along with an apple away from direct sunlight. The vapour from the apple will help to ripen the avocados.

Store garlic in a cool, dry place away from direct sunlight. Don't place it in the refrigerator or other foods will pick up the garlic flavour.

Don't store green ginger next to garlic as the ginger will dehydrate the garlic.

Never use an egg that has a broken or cracked shell, and avoid washing eggs because it will remove the protective outer layer, which slows moisture loss and keeps bacteria out.

Reduce the fat

Use lettuce leaves to remove fat from soups, gravy or stews. At the end of cooking place a few lettuce leaves in the pot with the soup, gravy or stew. The fat will cling to the leaves when you remove them.

Mayonnaise

I like to use the Kewpie brand of mayonnaise – a Japanese mayo that comes in a distinctive squeezy bottle. Look for it in supermarkets and Asian food stores.

How to kill a crayfish

To kill a crayfish quickly and painlessly, I recommend that you first place it in a freezer. The crayfish will 'go to sleep'. (Leave it in the freezer for an hour or so.) Then place the crayfish on a cutting board so that the tail curls towards the board. Flatten it out as much as possible, and with one hand grasp the tail where it joins the body. Holding a large kitchen knife in the other hand, position the point between the crayfish's eyes, with the blade facing away from the hand holding the tail. Press the point of the knife into the head, pressing firmly until it goes right through the crayfish's head to the cutting board, then bring the blade down firmly between the eyes.

Another option is to drown the crayfish in a pot of cold fresh water for about 30 minutes. Make sure the pot has a tight fitting lid as the crayfish will probably thrash about, drenching you in the process. Never put a live crayfish into boiling water.

Stocks

When I have time at home, I like to make my own stock. Here are my favourite recipes for chicken and fish stock, which can be frozen for later use.

Chicken Stock
2 kg chicken bones
4 litres water
½ kg vegetables (eg onion, carrot, celery, leek)
100ml dry white wine
1 sprig fresh thyme, or 1 tsp dried thyme
3 bay leaves
1 small bunch parsley
10 black peppercorns

Chop the chicken bones and place in a large pot. Cover the bones with cold water and bring to the boil. Drain and rinse the bones under cold water.

Clean the pot and put the bones back in along with the 4 litres of water. Peel and roughly chop the vegetables and add to the pot along with the wine, thyme, bay leaves, parsley and peppercorns. Bring to the boil and simmer gently for 6 hours.

The stock will evaporate, so after 1 hour add another 500ml of hot water. Skim the fat off the top and strain. Allow to cool.

Divide into zip-lock bags, measuring the amount that goes into each bag in millilitres and write this on the bag. Freeze for later use.

Fish Stock
50ml extra virgin olive oil
200g onions, sliced
2kg fish bones, well washed
4 litres water
100ml dry white wine
juice of ½ lemon
5 parsley stalks
4 white peppercorns

If you cook this stock for longer than 20 minutes the flavour will be bitter and the stock spoiled.

Place the oil in a saucepan with the onions and fish bones. Cook on a low heat for 5 minutes, then add the remaining ingredients and bring to the boil. Simmer for 20 minutes.

Remove from the heat, skim the fat off the top, strain and allow to cool.

Divide into zip-lock bags, measuring the amount that goes into each bag in millilitres and writing this on the bag. Freeze for later use.

GLOSSARY

Bocconcini
This cheese is the 'little brother' of mozzarella. Like mozzarella it is a fresh, semi-soft, white cheese made from the milk of water buffalo. Bocconcini is formed into small balls and is described by its Italian name, which means 'small mouthfuls'. (See also my 'five per cent magic ingredients', page 227.)

Canola oil
Canola oil is made from rapeseed. It is low in saturated fats and is a neutral oil suitable for frying at high temperatures.

Carnaroli rice
This Italian rice has a medium grain and a high starch content, which increases its absorption capacity, making it perfect for rice dishes that are cooked slowly, such as risotto. (See also my 'five per cent magic ingredients', page 227.)

Celery salt
This distinctive salt is made from finely ground celery seeds mixed with salt. It is a key ingredient in a Bloody Mary cocktail. Look for it in specialty food stores and good supermarkets.

Ciabatta
This is a light, crusty, Italian bread that comes in an elongated, slightly flat shape ('ciabatta' translated means 'slipper'). Its porous texture means it toasts easily and soaks up flavours well. It is delicious drizzled with extra virgin olive oil and lightly grilled.

Emmental
This is a Swiss cheese characterised by its marble-sized holes throughout the cheese. It has a firm, creamy texture and a slightly nutty flavour.

Manchego
This famous sheep's milk cheese from the La Mancha region of Spain is a rich, golden and firm and can be grated or shaved for salads. It is made from the milk of Manchega sheep and the cheese is aged for between 60 days and 2 years.

Mascarpone
Hailing from Italy's Lombardy region, mascarpone is a buttery-rich, double-cream to triple-cream cheese made from cow's milk. It is delicious served as an accompaniment to cakes and desserts. Look for it in the chiller at supermarkets.

Panko crumbs
These are breadcrumbs used in Japanese cooking. The crumbs are flakier than ordinary breadcrumbs and so when cooked create a lighter, crispier coating than ordinary breadcrumbs. You will find them in the Asian section of good supermarkets.

Parmigiano-Reggiano
This Italian hard, dry cheese is aged for a minimum of 18 months and has a sharp flavour. It is used in Italian cooking to impart additional flavour to dishes. (See also my 'five per cent magic ingredients', page 229.)

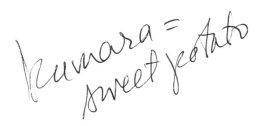

kumara = sweet potato

Pin-boning salmon

This is the process by which you remove the fine bones that run at an angle in a line down the length of a salmon fillet. Place salmon skin-side down on a board and use your fingertips to locate the pin bones, which protrude slightly through the flesh. Using a pair of fish-boning tweezers, gently extract the bones without damaging the flesh of the fish.

Shallot

Similar in appearance to a small, elongated onion, shallots divide into cloves like garlic when peeled. If a recipe calls for '1 shallot', use all the cloves. It has a milder flavour than onion.

Spanish smoked paprika

This paprika is indispensible in Spanish cooking. It is made from ground, smoked varieties of the *Capsicum annuum* pepper. It comes in varying intensities from mild to hot, and imparts a distinctive smoky flavour to your cooking. Don't be tempted to substitute ordinary paprika as this lacks the same smoky character. Available from www.souschef.co.nz.

Shreddo

This is a suet-based shortening commonly used these days in place of suet, which is made from beef fat. But don't be put off. Suet is an essential ingredient in pastry for traditional steak and kidney pudding as well as in steamed puddings, dumplings and Christmas mincemeat. Its high melting point helps to create a smooth, velvety pastry. Look for Shreddo in the baking aisle of your supermarket.

Tabasco chipotle sauce

Tabasco chipotle (pronounced *chee-poht-lay*) sauce is made from red jalapeños dried slowly over smouldering pecan wood to produce a full flavoured, spicy sauce with a dense, smoky flavour. It is available from www.souschef.co.nz.

Truffle oil

This flavoured oil is infused with truffles, and imparts the aroma and flavour of fresh truffles. It is delicious drizzled sparingly over dishes just before serving. (See also my 'five per cent magic ingredients', page 227.)

index

ACKNOWLEDGEMENTS

I'm fortunate to enjoy the enduring support of a tremendous group of colleagues, family and friends. To all of you, please know that I wouldn't be without you.

Special thanks go to my mum, Ellerie, and dad, Bryan, for gifting me a love of food. You taught me not to tolerate second best, and to be obsessive in the search for excellence. You have been there to support me every step of the way in all my crazy projects and new ventures. You are my staunchest critics, for which I thank you. I dedicate this book to you.

To my beautiful wife, Katrina, thank you for putting up with yet another project, and for giving me such honest feedback. You are my best friend and the love of my life.

Sarah, you are the most loyal sister, and a great support to me, Mum and Dad.

Special thanks go to my right-hand man and friend, Eugene Hamilton. You have worked tirelessly and shown me unstinting loyalty over the years, and I have you to thank for keeping me out of trouble most of the time. Thanks, too, to Darren Lim, another great chef and trusted colleague.

Thank you to my business partners, Richard Sigley, Phil Clark and Brian Fitzgerald, whose support is unwavering and who (almost) never question anything I do.

This book would not have happened without the brilliant photographer Kieran Scott. You are inspiring to work with, and you and your photographs tell it how it is. Thank you, too, to Tamara West for your creative eye and for interpreting my food with your sensitive styling.

I wouldn't have wanted to work with any editor other than Toni Mason. Thank you for persevering with Skype and for helping to shape my recipes for the home cook.

It has been wonderful to work with the team at Penguin Group (NZ). Thanks go to Debra Millar for her vision and patience when I got distracted by other projects; to Catherine O'Loughlin for her unrelenting attention to detail, and to Sarah Healey for her design.

And, finally, thanks to all those diners who keep coming back and who share with us their favourite dishes on our restaurant menus. You also keep us honest. Ultimately, this book is for you.

PENGUIN BOOKS

Published by the Penguin Group

Penguin Group (NZ), 67 Apollo Drive, Rosedale,
Auckland 0632, New Zealand (a division of Pearson New Zealand Ltd)
Penguin Group (USA) Inc., 375 Hudson Street,
New York, New York 10014, USA
Penguin Group (Canada), 90 Eglinton Avenue East, Suite 700, Toronto,
Ontario, M4P 2Y3, Canada (a division of Pearson Penguin Canada Inc.)
Penguin Books Ltd, 80 Strand, London, WC2R 0RL, England
Penguin Ireland, 25 St Stephen's Green,
Dublin 2, Ireland (a division of Penguin Books Ltd)
Penguin Group (Australia), 707 Collins Street, Melbourne,
Victoria 3008, Australia (a division of Pearson Australia Group Pty Ltd)
Penguin Books India Pvt Ltd, 11, Community Centre,
Panchsheel Park, New Delhi – 110 017, India
Penguin Books (South Africa) (Pty) Ltd, Block D, Rosebank Office Park,
181 Jan Smuts Avenue, Parktown North, Gauteng 2193, South Africa

Penguin Books Ltd, Registered Offices: 80 Strand, London, WC2R 0RL, England

First published by Penguin Group (NZ), 2012
10 9 8 7 6 5 4 3 2

Copyright © text, Simon Gault, 2013
Copyright © photographs, Kieran Scott, 2013

The right of Simon Gault and Kieran Scott to be identified as the author and
photographer of this work in terms of section 96 of the Copyright Act 1994 is
hereby asserted.

Designed and typeset by Sarah Healey, © Penguin Group (NZ)
Styling by Tamara West
Crown Lynn supplied by Alison Reid
Prepress by Image Centre, Ltd
Printed in China by 1010 Printing

ISBN 978-0-143-56862-9

A catalogue record for this book is available
from the National Library of New Zealand.

www.penguin.co.nz